COMMUNITY-ORIENTED POLICING FOR CVE CAPACITY

Adopting the Ethos through Enhanced Training

Nadia Gerspacher,
Motaz Al-Rababah,
Jessalyn Brogan Walker,
Nathaniel L. Wilson

Hedayah
countering violent extremism

ISBN: 978-1-6847-0892-5 (sc)
ISBN: 978-1-6847-0891-8 (e)

Library of Congress Control Number: 2019912657

Lulu Publishing Services rev. date: 09/20/2019

CONTENTS

PART II: THE CURRENT POLICE TRAINING CURRICULUM

PART III: MODULES FOR COP: SHIFTING THE ATTITUDE
AND BEHAVIOR OF POLICE INSTITUTIONS

PART IV: MODULES FOR COP: DEVELOPING INTERPERSONAL SKILLS

PART V: CONCLUSION

FOREWORD

It is with the utmost gratitude that I accepted the opportunity to write the foreward for the latest publications in the Community Policing for CVE program, a central pillar to the Hedayah organization since its inception in 2012. Hedayah, the International Center of Excellence for Countering Violent Extremism (CVE) was created in response to the growing desire from GCTF members and the wider international community to establish an independent, multilateral center devoted to capacity building programs, dialogue and communications, in addition to research and analysis to counter violent extremism in all of its forms and manifestations. We have become a center that can bring together experts, expertise, and experience from around the globe.

Shortly after the foundation of Hedayah, we began the fruitful collaboration with the United States Institute of Peace (USIP), with funding from the US Department of State Counter Terrorism Bureau. This partnership focused on providing a suite of trainings to a multitude of different front-line implementers to support their understanding of their role in CVE and furthering their ability to implement programming at the local level. Over the span of three years, the program engaged with civil society actors, educators, media representatives, government officials, and law enforcement from jointly identified priority countries who were directly experiencing the threat of violent extremism. Each bespoke engagement with law enforcement was designed to be both:

> *'philosophical'* – encouraging a change in institutional culture through acceptance that a reliance on

overly-coercive policing ultimately increases the threat by antagonising sentiments of mistrust in hostile communities; and,

'practical' – providing an opportunity for officers to formulate new approaches for dealing with key aspects of day to day policing such as on the ground presence in hostile communities, stop and search tactics, and engagement with minority groups.

The focus on law enforcement was of particular interest to our organization and me at the individual level. I was fortunate enough to be raised appreciating and recognizing what a community-oriented policing service looked like, as my mother was the first female police officer in the United Arab Emirates. I witnessed the strength of the relationships she was able to build with those in our community and the resultant trust that was bestowed upon her and colleagues in uniform. While there was the potential that this might result in privileged information being shared with her, it was more important to her that the people she was responsible for serving were confident in her ability to respond in times of need and with the appropriate levels of knowledge and understanding of the issue at hand.

In the Countering Violent Extremism (CVE) context, the transition to more community-based approaches is vital. There is clear evidence that actual or perceived overly-coercive policing approaches serve as a key driver of violent extremism. In areas where the police are seen as discriminatory, corrupt and/ or heavy-handed individuals, young people, especially from marginalized groups, will have an increased risk of radicalization and recruitment to VE groups. The community policing model allows for a reliable and mutual flow of information between the public and the police, as well as effective security partnerships with community leaders and local organizations.

The feedback from each of the trainings delivered by USIP and Hedayah indicated a strong appreciation for the knowledge disseminated as well as a desire for ongoing engagement at all levels within the policing infrastructure; from front line officers to those in a management position all the way to those with oversight over the entire police service. For this reason, when our partners at USIP proposed the idea of drafting the book in front of you, we fully supported the idea as a way to continue to support the work of those involved in curriculum and organizational reform efforts to promote a greater understanding and culture of community policing. By proposing additional knowledge and skills-based modules to be included in the new-recruit training curriculum, this material could be received and used by a much wider audience, ensuring that all officers understand their role as one of community policing, rather than relegating that responsibility to one specialized unit.

Upon being handed over wholly to the Hedayah Washington D.C. office in October 2017, the Community Policing for CVE program seeks to effect sustainable organizational and behavioral change in the police academy training of partnering countries. The material contained within this book has formed the cornerstone for this program and it is our sincere hope that it will continue to support the work of international law enforcement agencies and training academies as they strive to embed community policing principles into their academy curriculum to allow it to take root within their organization.

I want to express my sincere thanks to our colleagues at the United States Institute of Peace, particularly Dr. Nadia Gerspacher for initiating and overseeing this process through to publication. A special thanks as well to Mr. Patrick Lynch, Director of our D.C. office who oversaw the program transition from USIP to our first satellite office. As well, this would not have been possible without the generous funding contributions from our friends at the US State Department who financed the initial stages of this program and the drafting of this book, as well as the UK Foreign and Commonwealth Office who continue to support ongoing training initiatives, focused on reviewing and revising existing training approaches and curriculum. Finally, a huge appreciation to all of our partners in law enforcement who have worked alongside us in this program and in the drafting of this material. We thank you both for the courage of your daily work as well as in your ability to identify ways in which you can continue to improve your service to the community.

Maqsoud Kruse
Executive Director
Executive Office
Hedayah

PREFACE

A few things happened during the early 2010s that inspired the project from which this book springs. The first development was a growing recognition that terrorism could not be fought by military means alone (if at all), which in turn led to the emergence of a new approach to political violence and a new label for those engaging in it. "Countering violent extremism "(CVE) became a complement to, or in some cases the replacement for, counterterrorism policy, and those who had previously been called "terrorists" were now often referred to as "violent extremists." The emergence of CVE, which had a significant impact on programming both domestically and internationally turned the spotlight on the root causes of politically motivated violence and suggested that the push and pull factors that lead to radicalization and the carrying out of attacks need to be addressed if terrorism is going to be addressed in any meaningful way.

Many key actors in the fight against terrorism rallied around CVE. In 2011, the Global Counter Terrorism Fund (GCTF) was created as a platform to support the development of a new international infrastructure to fight terrorism by developing good practices and tools for policymakers and practitioners. Out of that initiative was born the first-ever "International Center of Excellence for Countering Violent Extremism," a hub for CVE research and the dissemination of good practices. Hosted by the United Arab Emirates, the new center was called Hedayah. Hedayah was created in response to the growing desire to enable members of the international community to share good practices and reflect together on CVE-related issues. Hedayah was tasked with developing several strands of programming to assist members with their CVE efforts. One of those strands was a policing program that would provide guidelines for countries facing the threat of violent extremism.

With support from the United States Department of State, the United States Institute of Peace (USIP) in Washington, DC, partnered with Hedayah to develop what became the Policing for CVE program. Since 2013, the program has developed tools for police institutions that have allowed them to contribute their country's CVE capacity. In guidelines made available to members of the GCTF, the program has identified various police practices as the source of grievances that have helped fuel radicalization and violent extremism. In CVE speak, some people have been pushed toward violent extremism by traditional law enforcement approaches and by policing practices that privilege the use of force, especially excessive force.

Police have a special position in the context of CVE. They can contribute significantly to the justification for violent extremism when they use, or are perceived to use, excessive force. Indeed, this approach sends signals about the relationship not just between the police and the community but between a government and its people. At the same time, police institutions can help weaken the arguments used by violent extremists by gaining the trust of d communities and acquiring legitimacy in the eyes of the public. In order to contribute to their country's CVE capacity, police forces need to adopt a different approach to policing, one that had once been of interest to many countries (including the United States, France, Pakistan, and the United Kingdom) but that had fallen out of favor because of the numerous challenges involved in trying to implement it. This approach is best known as "community policing," or "community-oriented policing." The problem set of CVE encouraged police forces to take a fresh look at community policing, which is ideally suited to tackling fluid and often invisible problems—such as the process of radicalization— in increasingly heterogeneous societies.

It became clear to many policymakers and policing experts that the ailing relationships between police institutions and the communities they are supposed to protect have to be addressed in a way that can help restore the social contract between government and citizens, especially members of marginalized communities. Countering violent extremism is really about developing a prevention capacity. Indeed, working on the root causes of radicalization that lead to violent extremism is essentially a preventive policy choice. Furthermore, to tackle CVE effectively requires a whole-of-government approach, even a whole-of-society approach, and CVE capacity is a vital component of such an approach.

To put these foundational beliefs into practice, USIP began to work hand in hand with Hedayah to develop a program that would help policing institutions develop their CVE capacity by adopting a community-oriented ethos. Community policing has been defined in many different ways and implemented in an equally wide variety of ways. The Policing for CVE Program insisted on embracing a new interpretation of community policing, one that emphasized the need for police forces to adopt an *ethos* of service to the community. The idea is that the police develop a mindset about their role in society as part of a government infrastructure and as part of society themselves. Their role is essentially to provide protection to the community as a whole and to its individual members. In order to provide protection from violent extremist groups and their activities, the police need to develop the skills to partner with members of the community and to work collaboratively to solve problems long before traditional law enforcement methods and the use of force would be required. And in order to adopt the community-oriented ethos, the entire police institution needs to integrate that ethos into its everyday decisions, strategies, policies, and operations.

The Policing for CVE Program built at USIP has developed a series of courses for police institutions interested in developing their CVE capacity, essentially identifying the effective strategies that can help them work closely with communities to address potential and emerging threats. The program, which was handed over to Hedayah to run in 2018, has developed and delivered a series of courses whose titles include:

- The Role of Police in CVE
- Community Policing for CVE
- Institutionalizing Community Policing for CVE: From Policy to Practice
- Assessing Police Capacity for Community Policing to Counter Violent Extremism

- Leveraging International Police Cooperation Organizations for Countering Violent Extremism
- Police Academy Curriculum Workshop
- Planning Workshop On Refining Pakistan's "Policing for Countering Violent Extremism" National Strategy and Implementation Plan

This idea for this book came to me during a course that I was delivering in Washington, DC, in 2016. Together with police leadership from Pakistan, Tunisia, and Jordan, I was engaged in a course to teach police academies how to assess their level of community orientation and how to develop a strategy to enhance their community involvement. It became evident that a book like this one would serve its audience well by highlighting the key knowledge and skills needed by officers in a community-oriented police institution. It also became clear that if the book was to inspire real change, it needed to go beyond explaining how to conduct assessments and also offer guidance on what changes are needed in existing police academy curricula. So, with support from the U.S. State Department and always in partnership with Hedayah, the Policing for CVE program this book began to take shape.

The Public Security Directorate of Jordan agreed to contribute to this project by accepting my invitation for Lt. Col. Al-Rababah to coauthor the book. He was instrumental in the analysis of the typical existing training curricula and in contextualizing policing as it is happening in many countries around the world. We enjoyed the support of our two other coauthors, who contributed their peacebuilding and criminology expertise to the book. Ms. Walker and Mr. Wilson were on my team and part of the entire Policing for CVE program and had a good grasp of the program's goals. After the analysis of existing curricula from Nigeria, Kenya, Jordan, Pakistan, Tunisia, and elsewhere, we applied several disciplines to the CVE problem set—including criminology, conflict resolution, psychology, and police reform—to construct a set of knowledge and skills necessary for police to have the capacity to partner and solve problems with communities. The solutions included in this book are informed by a variety of policing approaches, models, and theories.

As an assessment of the typical police academy training program revealed, many of the skills police officers and institutions need in order to build long-term partnerships with community members and develop a community-oriented mindset are not taught at the academies. This shortcoming is exacerbated by the fact that selection criteria for police recruits do not help identify individuals with the attributes needed to implement a community-oriented ethos. This book seeks to help police institutions not only identify these problems but also rectify them. It is available in French, English, and Arabic to ensure that it can be widely used.

Nadia Gerspacher
Washington, DC
June 2019

ACKNOWLEDGMENTS

This project as well as the Policing for CVE program would not have been possible without the support of the U.S. State Department's Bureau of Counterterrorism and Countering Violent Extremism. Its staff are to be applauded for recognizing that professionalizing the police force is an important way for countries to counter the threat of violent extremism. The bureau was a steady and reliable partner throughout the development of the Policing for CVE Program. Special thanks to Oliver Wilcox, Robert McKenzie, Hassan Abbassy, Ayhan Ucok, and Laurie Freeman for their support of the project and for helping to develop the theory of change that is the foundation of the project.

We are grateful to USIP for giving us the space and time to research, develop content and solutions, and write this manuscript. Thank you to Jeff Helsing for including the program and this project in the plans of USIP's Academy for International Conflict Management and Peacebuilding (which enabled this book to be written) and for his constant support.

Thank you to Jessalyn Brogan Walker for her tireless and always enthusiastic contributions, which ranged from administrative support to logistical expertise and editing prowess. Thank you to Nathaniel L. Wilson for his contributions since the beginning of the development of the Policing for CVE Program. Nate surmounted administrative, bureaucratic, political, and organizational hurdles to ensure that police officers from Jordan, Pakistan, Tunisia, Nigeria, Somalia, Kenya, Kosovo, Afghanistan, and many other countries were vetted and were able to travel to attend workshops held in Abu Dhabi, Italy, and Washington, DC.

A very sincere thank you also goes to the Public Security Directorate of Jordan for seconding Lt. Col. Al-Rababah to work with the program on this project for a year.

Special thanks to the police academies and their leadership who shared their existing training programs with the Policing for CVE Program. That information allowed us to understand the gaps and identify trends across countries to ensure that the book addresses the real need as the right level.

And most of all, thank you to all the police officers who enthusiastically participated in the program. We are grateful for their courage in discussing the challenges within and outside of their respective police institutions, their hard work that resulted in plans to adopt the community-oriented policing ethos, and their willingness to work with colleagues back at home to push forward new ways to fighting terrorism and violent extremism. To name them would not be prudent given their contexts, but they know who they are and we consider them part of the team.

ABOUT THE AUTHORS

Nadia Gerspacher is the former director of security sector education at the Academy for International Conflict Management of the United States Institute of Peace (USIP). Her portfolio included a capacity-building program that enabled her to develop best practices for both implementation and planning. She oversaw projects to identify and disseminate insights, guidelines, knowledge, and skills to security sector audiences in fragile, conflict-affected states. At USIP and elsewhere, she has developed numerous programs to support police reform efforts and security sector reform in general; and has contributed to many partnerships internationally to develop courses, conduct studies, and provide instruction to donor countries and security actors. Her publications include academic studies, technical guides, and applied research and studies to improve foreign assistance and policing practices. She has a PhD in international relations, her research focusing on international police cooperation and on the institutions that facilitate that cooperation. She has also conducted research on the capacity building of police institutions worldwide.

Motaz Al-Rababah is a retired colonel from the Public Security Directorate in Jordan. He has twenty-five years of domestic and international criminal justice experience as a project manager, mentor, consultant, educator, and trainer. A recognized expert in the fields of security sector reform, countering violent extremism, and community policing, in 2016 he began working for the United States Institute of Police on the program that led to this book. Previously, he was an instructor at the Royal Police Academy teaching new recruits and advanced and specialized training programs. Prior to that assignment, he worked as an instructor and liaison officer for the Anti-Terrorism Assistant Program at the Jordanian International Centre for Police Training. He served as a United Nations police adviser in peacekeeping operations for three years in Kosovo, Haiti, and Liberia. His educational experience includes a PhD in political science focusing on countering violent extremism; a master's degree in counter terrorism; a master's degree in international conflict resolution; and a bachelor's degree in law and police science.

Jessalyn Brogan Walker is the program manager of the Community Policing for CVE program at Hedayah and Programs Officer at the Global Center on Cooperative Security. In this position, she works with international police trainers, officers, and leadership to promote community policing as a tool to counter violent extremism. They collaborate to determine opportunities for revising existing in-country police academy curricula to incorporate a community-oriented ethos throughout the training. During her time at the United States Institute of Peace in 2014–2017, she supported the capacity-building program with Hedayah to organize and deliver a host of CVE-relevant workshops and trainings with law enforcement, government, and civil society actors. She holds an undergraduate degree in sociology and politics and a master's degree in criminology from the University College Cork, where she graduated in 2013. Her research interests include international root causes of crime and violence, global prison systems, and identity sensitivity and appreciation.

Nathaniel L. Wilson joined the United States Institute of Peace (USIP) in 2011after stints with the Partnership for Global Security in Washington, DC, and at the Mossawa Center in Haifa, Israel. At USIP, he has coordinated education and training on countering violent extremism (CVE); implemented a project to develop and deliver a CVE curriculum to key civil society and government actors; and coordinated the Policing for CVE program. As the Libya country manager, he leads efforts to support key institutions and build local capacity to undertake peacebuilding and contribute to stabilization and reconciliation in

Libya. He has been published in numerous forums and by various institutions, including the Strategic Studies Institute & U.S. Army War College Press and USIP. He holds a master's degree in international relations from American University's School of International Service and a bachelor's degree in political science from the University of Missouri-St. Louis.

GLOSSARY OF TERMS

Countering violent extremism (CVE) refers to the programs and policies for countering and preventing radicalization and recruitment into violent extremism and terrorism as part of an overall counter-terrorism strategy and framework. This definition is inclusive of strategic, non-coercive counterterrorism programs and policies including those involving education and broad-based community engagement; more targeted narrative/messaging programs and counter-recruitment strategies; disengagement and targeted intervention programs for individuals engaging in radicalization; as well as de-radicalization, disengagement and rehabilitation programs for former violent extremist offenders.

Counterterrorism (CT) is the realm of coercive and non-coercive programs and policies to prevent and deny opportunities for violent extremist activity and to disrupt, arrest, prosecute, and/or kill violent extremist groups and individuals.

Deviance describes an action or behavior that violates social norms; it may or may not involve committing a crime

Factors contributing to radicalization are circumstances that can contribute to individual's engagement in violent extremism.

Radicalization leading to violent extremism (RLVE) is the process through which an individual to an increasing extent accepts the use of violent means, in an attempt to reach a specific political, religious or ideological objective

Terrorism is any action that is intended to cause death or serious bodily harm to civilians or non-combatants, when the purpose of such an act, by its nature or context, is to intimidate a population, or to compel a Government or an international organization to do or to abstain from doing any act.

Violent extremism represents the final stage of the radicalization process, and refers to the beliefs and actions of people who support or use ideologically motivated violence to further political, religious or ideological objectives. In other words, violent extremists do not only comprise individuals who are willing to embrace physical violence but also individuals who actively support, recruit or advocate in favor of a violent extremist ideology

CHAPTER 1
INTRODUCTION

Awareness and fear of terrorism and violent extremism have grown exponentially in the past two decades, leading to the emergence of a host of approaches intended to prevent, counter, and respond to this potent threat. Given the nature and scope of violent extremism, any strategy to counter it must be multifaceted to be effective. Although everyone within a society should play a part in maintaining a safe environment, no one plays a more visible and scrutinized role than the police service. Police act within the community while enforcing the law as determined by other government agencies. Frontline officers can have a profound impact on informing national policies and action. However, that ability is predicated on the community having trust and confidence in the police service to act and interact in a fair and equitable way.

To understand and counter the threat that modern terrorism and violent extremism pose to citizens, both government and nongovernment actors must acquire new knowledge and practices. To effectively provide protection to their communities, police must adopt practices and a mindset that privileges a proximity to the communities they aim to serve. This proximity is achieved through the establishment of partnerships between police and their communities as well as with other government and nongovernment partners, which in collaboration can act as a formidable obstacle to violent extremism and terrorism. With mutually beneficial partnerships in place, communities and police can proactively address problems that might lead to violent extremism. To enjoy legitimacy, police need to adopt an ethos that will transform the policing organization into one that is community centered. These practices are embodied in the philosophy known as "community-oriented policing," or COP.

Adopting a COP ethos requires a commitment to increased transparency, cooperation with community representatives, unbiased respect in communication and interaction with citizens, and a focus on understanding and solving local problems. A COP ethos fosters a reliable and mutual flow of information between the public and the police, as well as effective security partnerships with community leaders and organizations.

In the countering violent extremism (CVE) context, a transition to more community-based approaches is vital. Ample evidence demonstrates that the use of excessive force by police, together with biased or discriminatory policing, may be key factors in the Radicalization leading to Violent Extremism (RLVE) process of some members of the community and the creation of tacit support for violence among other community members. These lessons have been observed by many police services throughout the world, and they are striving to find a balance between, on the one side, effective law enforcement and the provision of protection and, on the other side, a closer connection to the communities they serve.

To institutionalize a COP approach, the police service must emphasize a community orientation from the police recruitment stage and continuously reinforce it throughout the academy training process. The culture of the police academy must align with the approach of police officers in the field, making it essential that lessons taught at the academy are grounded in real-life examples. Although the cultural component of the learning environment is critical, so too are knowledge- and skills-based lessons that support and promote a community orientation so that, when they enter into active service, officers are equipped to work with and for the community they serve, improving their personal and institutional reputations and promoting community safety.

This book builds on the experience and expertise of the United States Institute of Peace and the Hedayah Centre of Excellence in Countering Violent Extremism, which have trained police leadership from throughout the Middle East, Africa and the Balkans in community policing for CVE. Through assessing international police academy curricula, the book contends that existing training programs for recruits and officers do not support a

COP ethos and can impede the ability of officers to interact proactively with their communities. With the goal of encouraging international law enforcement training institutions to change their attitudes and approaches, the book introduces knowledge- and skills-based modules of instruction that can be included in an academy's curriculum, as well as principles and good practices to support the development of a community-oriented ethos throughout a police service.

Part I of the book explores the current international policing context and introduces key themes around COP. It defines the meaning of a COP ethos in a police service and describes how this definition differs from the existing approach to policing, which reflects the historic militarization of the police. In addition, it presents some of the ongoing challenges to adopting the COP approach into the policing culture, from both an institutional and an individual level.

Part II focuses on current training programs, examining the types of material covered and the time allotted to various topics. Following this assessment, the impact of existing training on police behavior and community attitudes toward the police is analyzed.

Parts III and IV present modules of knowledge- and skills-based learning that can be included in a national curriculum to promote a COP ethos throughout the police service. These modules can help police recruits to recognize the importance of earning public confidence, understanding the root causes of violence, and supporting diverse identities. Other modules provide a grounding in problem solving skills, communication skills such as strategic listening and public speaking, and conflict resolution skills such as negotiation and mediation.

The volume concludes with a discussion of the impact of the proposed augmented curriculum on police–community relations and CVE efforts.

Although this subject matter is likely to be of interest to those throughout the policing institution and those concerned with preventing and countering violent extremism, this book is directed specifically at those in charge of police academy curricula and police academy instructors. It presents the information needed to advocate for curriculum reform, and provides material and thematic support to tailor existing police academy curricula to support a community orientation throughout the entire police service.

PART I

FROM PARAMILITARY TO COMMUNITY-ORIENTED POLICING

CHAPTER 2
CURRENT CONTEXT

Governments often respond to a threat of violent extremist attack by issuing legislation that gives police additional powers to combat potential attacks. More than 140 governments have passed counterterrorism legislation since September 11, 2001.[1] This emergency-driven approach has given police authority to deploy heavy-handed tactics even though violent extremists have long been successful in deliberately provoking the state into an overreaction to the threat posed by terrorism.[2]

In authorizing heavy-handed responses, governments fall into a trap laid by violent extremists who hope to plant fear and give rise to a more forcible response than is justified. This response feeds into the cycle of violence on which violent extremism flourishes.[3] This book offers alternative approaches to misplaced heavy-handed police tactics that

---

[1] Human Rights Watch, "In the Name of Security: Counterterrorism Laws Worldwide since September 11," *Human Rights Watch*, June 29, 2012, https://www.hrw.org/report/2012/06/29/name-security/counterterrorism-laws-worldwide-september-11.

[2] Tom Parker, "It's a Trap: Provoking an Overreaction Is Terrorism 101," *RUSI*, June 18, 2015, https://rusi.org/publication/rusi-journal/it's-trap-provoking-overreaction-terrorism-101.

[3] The Tunisian government declared a state of emergency on November 2015 as a response to terrorist attacks in certain cities. The French government became increasingly reliant on its emergency powers in 2015 and 2016 as a response to terrorist attacks in Paris and Nice. See Anne-Sylvie Chassany, "France: The Permanent State of Emergency," *Financial Times,* October 2, 2017.

are so problematic. Before entertaining alternatives, however, we must understand why police resort to such tactics in the first place.

Militarization of the Police

Police often use their equipment as a tool intended to ensure or restore the safety of both themselves and the public. Yet, violent extremists and other actors who threaten security are often armed with greater firepower than police have access to. Many police institutions note that the military-style weapons that violent extremist organizations (VEOs) use have changed considerably in recent years. Many in the policing community believe that neutralizing such a threat and responding to an attack requires paramilitary equipment. Proponents of this view call for advanced equipment and weapons to better position police to respond to violent extremist threats.

The problem with this approach lies in the excessive use of violence to respond to unrest or security threats. Police violence may be seen as unfair, unjust, and disproportionate by communities, and its use costs police officers their perceived legitimacy and community trust. Although concerns for the safety of officers may be a justification for heavy-handed tactics, this strategy tends to do more harm than good, especially in CVE situations where much of the activity that leads to the use of violence is not necessarily criminal and thus outside the scope of traditional policing.

A Lack of Legitimacy

A lack of real or perceived procedural justice has a significant impact on the public's willingness to grant legitimacy to the police and their use of force.[4] Procedural justice is the concept that fairness should be one of the principles that guides a criminal justice system. Furthermore, a willingness to cooperate with the police, a key component of COP, is affected by

---

[4] Jonathan Jackson et al., "Monopolizing Force? Police Legitimacy and Public Attitudes toward the Acceptability of Violence," *Psychology, Public Policy, and Law* 19, no. 4 (May 2013): 479–497.

individual experiences with police.[5] There is a negative correlation between police use of excessive, unwarranted violence and perceived police legitimacy.[6] Police legitimacy is the community's recognition that the police hold the statutory right to enforce laws. Lack of police legitimacy may increase public resistance and hostility to being policed, does not promote voluntary compliance, and discourages cooperation with police.

When police officers respond to nonviolent protests as though they are potential threats to public safety, rather than recognize that people are exercising their rights, the community may view the police response as unwarranted. Such reactions are more likely to make citizens view police as a part of the institutions that they are protesting against rather than as part of their own community. Community members' perception of how police officers treat them influences their willingness to comply with instruction from authority.

In a paradoxical environment of enhanced emergency power and a call to develop relationships with communities, many police institutions invest most of their training resources in teaching recruits how to handle firearms, drive, apply first aid, and defend themselves, as well as other use-of-force tactics, even though only 10 percent of their duties on the job will put them in a position where they need to use these skills.[7]

Heavy-handed tactics reduce the distinction between a police officer and a soldier.[8] Unlike their military counterparts, police officers are granted (and trained) to exercise discretion on an ad hoc basis when they encounter disorder. Trained officers must have the capacity to de-escalate or otherwise address a situation on their own without a preplanned approach developed by a commanding structure. Police officers are expected to make

---

[5] Tom R. Tyler and Jeffrey Fagan, "Legitimacy and Cooperation: Why Do People Help the Police Fight Crime in Their Communities?" *Ohio State Journal of Criminal Law* 6 (2006): 231–275.

[6] Jackson et al., "Monopolizing Force?"

[7] Allison T. Chappell, "Police Academy Training: Comparing Across Curricula," *Policing: An International Journal of Police Strategies & Management* 31, no. 1 (August 29, 2007): 36–56.

[8] A soldier follows orders and seldom employs discretion, whereas discretion within policing is critical to both the functioning of the police department and its relationship with the community it serves.

significant decisions regarding the freedom and safety of those with whom they interact. As the very foundation of police authority, legitimacy is a necessary condition to justify police use of force. When a police force has legitimacy, individuals understand why police have the right to exercise power and why citizens have a corresponding duty to comply.[9]

Heavy-Handed Policing Strengthens Extremism

Traditional policing responses to the violent extremist threat might include conducting surveillance, gathering information from informants, and excessive or illegitimate use of force or threatening to use force. Such an approach, without pre-existing trust from the community, may actually support the political messages of VEOs. The possible effects of this approach on the public can be a lack of interest in cooperating with the police, reluctance to solicit police assistance, and decreased motivation to inform police about suspicious activities.

For example, the practice of profiling can help violent extremist messages gain resonance. In many countries, minorities perceive police as targeting them,[10] leading them to be less resistant to violent extremist messages.[11] Furthermore, police officers who discriminate contribute to radicalization and even to the decision of VEOs to launch attacks.

A police overreaction under the guise of countering violent extremism is more likely to produce grievances and anger and to escalate violence than to promote a more peaceful society. "Hard policing" may be a short-term solution for reassuring a scared public, but it often gives rise to grievances that foment more violence. For many violent extremists, particularly leaders and ideologues, exposure to government repression

---

[9] Tom R. Tyler, "Psychological Perspectives on Legitimacy and Legitimation," *Annual Review of Psychology* 57, no. 1 (February 2006): 375–400.

[10] Farrukh B. Hakeem et al., *Policing Muslim Communities: Comparative International Context* (New York: Springer, 2012).

[11] Sarah Lyons-Padilla, Michele J. Gelfand, Hedieh Mirahmadi, Mehreen Farooq, and Marieke van Egmond, "Belonging Nowhere: Marginalization and Radicalization Risk Among Muslim Immigrants, *Behavioral Science and Policy* (December 2015), https://behavioralpolicy.org/wp-content/uploads/2017/05/BSP_vol1is2_-Lyons-Padilla.pdf.

and torture by police and other security forces are significant factors in their radicalization.[12] Excessive use of police force and degrading treatment are drivers that can contribute to an individual's journey toward violent extremism. In a 2016 study commissioned by the Network for Religious and Traditional Peacemakers, 119 interviews were conducted with former Boko Haram fighters. Only 9 percent of respondents identified religion as their main incentive; revenge against security forces' brutality was cited by 57 percent.[13]

Heavy-handed tactics have been associated with the abuse of human rights and a lack of oversight that can make people reluctant to cooperate with police officers. These tactics may also lead people to view the police not as protectors of their security or their rights but as forces of repression that are open to manipulation by the government and want to suppress domestic opposition in the name of national security. A Human Rights Council report published in 2015 notes that the threat of terrorism has been used to legitimize far-reaching infringements of civil liberties during protests.[14] Human rights violations by security forces are recognized by the UN Global Counterterrorism Strategy as conducive to the spread of terrorism,[15] a point of view endorsed by Ban Ki-Moon when he was UN secretary-general:

> Governments that exhibit repressive and heavy-handed
> security responses in violation of human rights and the
> rule of law, such as profiling of certain populations,
> adoption of intrusive surveillance techniques and

---

[12] United States Agency for International Development (USAID), prepared by Guilain Denoeux, *Guide to the Drivers of Violent Extremism* (Washington, DC: USAID, February 2009), https://pdf.usaid.gov/pdf_docs/Pnadt978.pdf.

[13] Office of the United Nations High Commissioner for Human Rights, "Terrorism and Counter-terrorism," Factsheet 32 (July 2008), https://www.ohchr.org/Documents/Publications/Factsheet32EN.pdf.

[14] Christof Heyns, "Report of the Special Rapporteur on Extrajudicial, Summary or Arbitrary Executions," UN Human Rights Council, April 1, 2014; and UN Secretary General, "Promotion and Protection of Human Rights, Including Ways and Means to Promote the Human Rights of Migrants," August 3, 2015.

[15] UN General Assembly, "UN Global Counter-Terrorism Strategy," 2006.

prolongation of declared states of emergency, tend to generate more violent extremists.[16]

The Role of Incarceration

When police officers charge ordinary, low-level criminals with terrorism-related offenses, they play into the hands of those looking to recruit vulnerable individuals into VEOs. How a criminal is classified determines how—if he or she is convicted and sentenced—the inmate is housed when incarcerated. An inmate may begin his or her journey in prison as a result of having committed a petty crime, but he or she may be radicalized by interactions with violent extremists and by real or perceived mistreatment at the hands of prison officials.

Indeed, the physical and emotional trauma endured by inmates has been shown to result in increased susceptibility to the narratives espoused by violent extremist recruiters. Many violent extremist groups find prisoners to be an attentive audience for their messages. Many examples could be cited. One of the men who attacked the *Charlie Hebdo* offices in Paris in 2015 was radicalized in a prison in France.[17] In 1995, Abu Muhammad Al–Maqdisi, was sentenced to fifteen years imprisonment for terrorist activities. During his incarceration, he spread radicalization messages and sought out inmates who would support violent extremist ideologies and activities. His most famous recruit was Abu Musab Al Zarqawi, who later became the leader of al-Qaeda in Iraq.[18] When police house criminals in facilities that lack rehabilitation programs, the risk of inmate radicalization increases. These inmates can subsequently influence the views of their friends and families on the outside.

---

[16] UN Secretary General, "Plan of Action to Prevent Violent Extremism," December 24, 2015.

[17] Haeyoun Park et al., "Charlie Hebdo Attackers' Path to Radicalization," *New York Times*, January 17, 2015.

[18] Ben Kesling and Suha Ma'ayeh, "Jordan Releases Zarqawi's Spiritual Mentor From Prison," *Wall Street Journal*, June 16, 2014.

Conclusion

Many police institutions claim that they have adopted community policing approaches when in reality they still rely on heavy-handed tactics. The use of force can play an important part in policing. However, police work does not have to be about the use or misuse of force; it can be about a partnership with the community to solve problems that can lead to violence. Indeed, it is becoming apparent that some traditional tactics have a negative impact on the efforts of police, as more aggressive tools translate into more aggressive policing. Seemingly indiscriminate responses and overreliance on the use and show of force leave police services enjoying less legitimacy in the eyes of their communities, thereby distancing them from those they should be protecting. Heavy-handed tactics may undermine community trust in police and reduce the level of community cooperation.

CHAPTER 3
COMPONENTS AND IMPACT OF COP

Heavy-handed policing approaches in many parts of the world have caused significant damage both to the legitimacy of the police and to the nature and scope of collaboration between the police and the people they aim to protect. Forceful approaches afford credibility to the grievance-based arguments of extremists and create fertile ground in which VEOs can take root. This chapter focuses on COP as a means of restoring and improving police legitimacy. It also addresses the issue of adopting a COP ethos throughout an entire police infrastructure. The chapter begins by explaining the COP philosophy, then discusses each of the three key the components of a COP approach, and concludes with an overview of how COP can aid efforts to counter violent extremism.

The Case for COP

COP as a philosophy illustrates the ways in which police can respond to community challenges through partnerships, organizational support, and a problem-solving approach. Fundamentally, COP is about establishing and maintaining mutual trust so police officers can demonstrate how they contribute to a community's security challenges. COP is not solely focused on reducing the crime rate in specific areas. The management of crime is one component of community safety, but many other issues affect communities. Adopting a COP ethos calls for police to support an approach that focuses on mitigation and prevention. The evolution in policing practices that is necessary to embrace a COP ethos takes into consideration the root causes of issues that may arise in communities, and requires police to devote time to analyzing specific conflicts and identifying long-term viable solutions.

Modern police need to be capable of serving increasingly diverse communities. If efforts are not made to understand and welcome people from various diverse backgrounds into their new environment, communities face a greater risk of being radicalized and recruited into violent extremism.[1] COP is a means of addressing the "us-versus-them" problem, as well as being an antidote to the current emphasis on responding only to immediate crimes.

In the context of violent extremism, COP addresses the factors that may contribute to people to joining VEOs, introducing dynamics based on communication and collaboration between the police and the people they protect. This is especially important in contexts in which traditions and legacies of distrust have reigned or where grievances are deeply ingrained in the attitudes and beliefs of the community, making community members reluctant to engage police. One requirement of a COP ethos is a collaborative relationship between police officers and individuals, one that prioritizes service over fighting crime. This relationship requires the entire police structure to have the knowledge and skills to address community issues in a constructive manner.

Steady and consistent communication between the police and the community makes both parties feel comfortable and empowered to interact with "the other" (i.e., a subgroup or a community within society that has different values, norms, and possibly habits than oneself). Police officers must be strategic and, instead of using heavy-handed tactics, seek mutually beneficial interactions with the community that focus on building relationships. This is what distinguishes COP from other approaches such as intelligence-led policing, which involves police interacting with the community solely through the use of surveillance technology and in search

---

[1] Mitchell F. Rice, "Policing Culturally-Linguistically Diverse Communities in an Era of Terrorism: Improving Community Policing as a Counter-Terrorism Strategy at the Grassroots Community Police Level," *NATO Science for Peace and Security Series, E: Human and Societal Dynamics* 125 (2016): 212–220.

of intelligence from informants. An example of intelligence-led policing is the CompStat system created by the New York Police Department in the late 1990s. The CompStat system computerizes statistical crime information that enables police to see crime trends as they happen in almost real time, allowing officers to implement crime response strategies promptly.[2] This approach is less useful than COP, especially when it comes to preventing violent extremism, because it ignores internal and external factors that may lead someone to commit that type of crime. COP focuses on crime prevention rather than deterrence by a show of force, as well as partnership building and maintenance and problem solving.

Communities want information on possible threats to their security. One avenue for this information is established and trusted channels of communication with the police. COP emphasizes community collaboration and partnership building rather than focusing purely on the criminal environment. When it is well implemented, COP delivers a regular stream of information that flows to and from the police and community. This communication educates all parties about incidences that may be precursor activities to violence and behaviors that can indicate violence is imminent. Communities need to have confidence in the police capacity to handle information correctly, to sustain a community partnership, and to address the threat of violence, whether it is imminent or not.

Components of COP

Community policing is not a single tactic or a set of specific procedures but rather a philosophical, institutional approach to how policing should be carried out.[3] The adoption of this ethos should be agency-wide and cover all police activities and the organizational culture of the entire police institution. COP officers work to strengthen their relationship with the

---

[2] James J. Willis et al., "The Co-Implementation of Compstat and Community Policing," *Journal of Criminal Justice* 38, no. 5 (2010): 969–980.
[3] Sarah Lawrence and Bobby McCarthy, "What Works in Community Policing?" Chief Justice Earl Warren Institute on Law and Social Policy, University of California Berkeley School of Law (November 2013), https://www.law.berkeley.edu/files/What_Works_in_Community_Policing.pdf.

community and help organize events that aim to increase security awareness. However, simply creating a special unit and assigning community policing officers is not as effective an approach as the adoption of an ethos. If only select officers are tasked with COP work while others continue to employ hard policing tactics, the message of one unit is negated by the work of the other, reducing the credibility and legitimacy of the police service as a whole.

A community-oriented service is increasingly seen as an approach that promises to enable police to get ahead of the threats and activities of violent extremist groups. One example is the PREVENT program in the United Kingdom, which has emphasized COP principles for preventing violent extremism.[4]

COP is made up of three components: problem solving, partnerships, and organizational transformation. Police must build partnerships and mutually trusting relationships with different public and private sectors, as well as with their communities, to address problems that have deep roots in society such as violent extremism and legacies of violence.[5] COP can make a tangible and durable contribution to broader strategic efforts to prevent terrorism and counter violent extremists even if policing approaches are not a stand-alone tool for CVE. COP should be implemented along with other local and national programs in a comprehensive strategy to combat terrorism in all its forms and manifestations, as well as to tackle the root causes that are exploited by violent extremists.[6]

Problem Solving

A key component of COP is problem solving. When problems come to the attention of the police, police have the opportunity to mitigate

---

[4] Secretary of State for the Home Department, "Prevent Strategy." HM Government, June 2011; and "The Prevent Strategy: A Guide for Local Partners in England." HM Government, May 2008.

[5] Dennis J. D. Sandole, "The 'New' Terrorism: Causes, Conditions and Conflict Resolution" (January 2004).

[6] Organization for Security and Co-Operation in Europe, "Preventing Terrorism and Countering Violent Extremism and Radicalization That Lead to Terrorism: A Community-Policing Approach," February 2014.

them and identify solutions. For rank-and-file officers and leadership to operationalize problem solving, police officers must be capable of thinking critically to address problems. Problem solving is not applicable only in situations involving crimes already in progress; it is a broad term that explains how to address particular problems or concerns by identifying them and finding the most appropriate response to solve or to reduce the problem.[7] Problem solving is the application of new approaches instead of continuing to use the same approaches. Police officers should avoid responding in a rote, mechanical fashion to different situations; the same response seldom produces different results. When police want to address a problem, they will be more effective if they can identify and deal with the underlying issues rather than simply reacting to the incident at hand.

There are many examples of effective uses of problem solving. The downtown area of Amman, Jordan, struggled with prostitution in the early 2000s. In response to complaints from local business owners and community members, police arrested women and sent them to jail, where they were then tried by local judges, typically released, and told to relocate to a different part of the city. In doing so, police simply pushed the problem to another area—they did not focus on the root causes of the crime. Eventually, an undercover female police officer started to ask questions within this targeted community about what made these women choose this path.[8] This line of communication helped to develop a sense of rapport between the women and the officer. Over months of investigation and discussion, the officer determined that arresting women and putting them in jail (from which they might emerge radicalized, angry, and violent) was not a solution to the underlying problem. Upon completion of a comprehensive investigation, police and social workers made a recommendation that was sent to the local magistrate. The judge used this recommendation to provide social services and support to each woman based on her particular needs rather than simply sending them all to jail. Using problem-solving skills, one officer changed the way the police force dealt with prostitution in the community.

Police officers need to acquire specific skills to become better problem

---

[7] James J. F. Forest, *Homeland Security: Protecting America's Targets,* vol. 2 (Westport, CT: Praeger Security International, 2006), 201.

[8] Anecdotal evidence from interview with Jordanian police officer.

solvers. Strong communication and analytical skills assist officers not only in identifying problems but also in exploring underlying causes of problems and determining the best ways to approach them. Police training should encourage creative thinking and exploration of alternatives, which will improve the problem-solving and decision-making skills for frontline officers.[9] According to *Problem-Oriented Policing*, a book by a leading scholar of crime prevention Anthony Braga, police officers should have appropriate analytical skills to screen, analyze, respond to, and assess problems.[10] These skills will help officers develop strategies that prevent and reduce crime (as discussed in part IV of this book). [11]

Skilled police officers can screen violent extremist threats and identify their root causes and vulnerable groups. Because of extensive daily interactions with community members, police are in the best position to identify grievances within the community and recognize vulnerable people. Police officers who have problem-solving skills including, but not limited to, communication skills—listening and asking the right questions—can encourage people to talk about their concerns.

Police officers should question the way they use their power and if it may cause harm and distress to the community, such as the use of force in making arrests or dealing with traffic violations. Heavy-handed tactics may give terrorists more credence in the eyes of individuals who had previously not been radicalized, as they identify a common enemy in the forceful behavior of the police.[12] Police officers with an understanding of the push and pull factors that may lead people to be recruited into criminal or extremist activity are better equipped to challenge those narratives. Through partnership and problem solving, police can address these factors (especially those directly related to police) and work toward solving them. Police with good communication skills can—in cooperation with other

---

[9] Rajnish Kumar Rai, "A Participatory Action Research Training Initiative to Improve Police Effectiveness," *Action Research* 10, no. 3 (2012): 225–243.

[10] Anthony A. Braga, *Problem-Oriented Policing and Crime Prevention*, 2nd ed. (Monsey, NY: Criminal Justice Press, 2008).

[11] Ibid.

[12] Henry Shaftoe, "Dealing with Terrorist Threats through a Crime Prevention and Community Safety Approach," *Crime Prevention and Community Safety* 9, no. 4 (October 24, 2007): 291–307.

stakeholders from the government and civil society—also advise the public on possible ways to address the drivers of extremism, even when an issue rests outside police authority or capabilities.

Partnership Building

Police do not have the capacity to address all the many drivers of violent extremism. Thus, effective partnerships and collaboration between police and different segments of the community are critical. In a true partnership, all sides agree to work together to improve the quality of life and to address community concerns. Police acknowledge and prioritize the needs and concerns of the public (such as speeding cars and the safety of play areas and parking lots) over issues that the police have historically prioritized. To foster a sense of partnership, police should treat every encounter that the public has with them as a teachable moment and use their position within the community not only to protect personal relationships but also to increase the general population's knowledge and awareness of public safety and possible threats. This includes, but is not limited to, interactions with local businesses, schools, social clubs and places of worship.

Preventing violent extremist incidents requires effective partnerships with the community and systematic and regular community interaction with police and other government actors. Police should be encouraged to open channels of communication within their jurisdiction and share knowledge with various actors across the community. Joint activities that make citizens feel responsible for challenging the threat of violent extremism are crucial.[13] Building partnership requires police to focus on developing preventive action plans that cover community concerns and address all forms of violence.[14]

Typically, the majority of contact that police have with the public occurs at the response stage, a situation that is likely to involve a heightened emotional state. These times are rarely the most propitious opportunities for relationship building, especially if community members feel the responding officers are unapproachable. With COP, the police and the community work together to address crime and quality-of-life issues, build

---

[13] Ibid.

[14] Ibid.

relationships, and get to know each other when things are going well. This ensures that when things are difficult or when there is an emergency, people know who to call and have a trusted point of contact in addition to any emergency services available.

In establishing and sharing problem-solving responsibilities with the community, the police service creates space for the community to contribute to problem solving, not just to point out problems. Well-maintained partnerships enable police to engage with all individuals in identifying possible threats and infrastructure vulnerabilities. When they undertake relationship-building efforts, officers find significant benefits in getting to know and working with local leaders and business owners, paving the way for police to request the assistance of these respected community figures when conflict is identified. Members of the community who assist police in resolving community problems through mediation and negotiation improve the image of police in the eyes of the community—by involving third parties, police aim to resolve the conflict rather than arrest people. Over time, the community comes to understand that community members also have a role to play in prevention.

A collaborative relationship between police and their community is essential to resolving local issues.[15] Both police and community members might be aware of people who are at risk of violent extremist recruitment. Collaborative relationships can facilitate linking those in need with services and resources that exist in the community—police can put those people in touch with community stakeholders who are best suited to address the at-risk individuals' issues. For example, police can ask community stakeholders such as school principals or doctors to see individuals who may want or need to go back to school or need medical or psychological treatment. Police are often aware of community members' needs but are not in the best position or equipped to address them. In creating connections with the community, police shift from the traditional model of policing and paramilitary tactics to an approach that is based on increasing trust and communication between law enforcement and the

---

[15] Michael S. McCampbell, *The Collaboration Toolkit for Community Organizations: Effective Strategies to Partner with Law Enforcement* (Washington, DC: U.S. Department of Justice, Office of Community Oriented Policing Services, 2014).

public.[16] Recognition of the fact that the police cannot solve community problems alone and need the assistance of their community highlights the key difference between the ethos of heavy-handed approaches and community policing. The traditional paradigm places police at the center of crime-fighting activities, seeing them as the only responsible institution for protecting the population; COP envisions the police service as one of many organizations responsible for reducing the threat of criminal activity – to include violent extremism- and promoting public safety.

To develop significant CVE capacity, police should seek opportunities to forge relationships with communities that are isolated and promote their participation in a conversation with the wider community so their voices are heard. This will ensure that the challenges of often overlooked populations are also considered and solutions are vetted at all levels.

Organizational Transformation

Typical police organizations have an organizational structure that tends to privilege the law enforcement culture of traditional policing.[17] COP encourages making profound changes in the police department's structure and applying modern management practices to foster officers' productivity and effectiveness.[18] Police should consider some specific changes to support COP, including in the realms of leadership, organizational evaluation, hierarchical culture, police academy training, in-service training, and recruitment policies. Organizational transformation will lead to changes in mindsets and skills, which in turn will lead to changes in how police officers behave.[19]

Police leadership must introduce a new ethos, new policies, and new practices to implement COP. The commitment of top leadership to COP

---

[16] John Murray, "Policing Terrorism: A Threat to Community Policing or Just a Shift in Priorities?" *Police Practice and Research* 6, no. 4 (2006): 347–361.

[17] J. Kevin Ford, "Building Capability throughout a Change Effort: Leading the Transformation of a Police Agency to Community Policing," *American Journal of Community Psychology* 39, no. 3–4 (June 2007): 321–334.

[18] U.S. Department of Justice Office of Community Oriented Policing Services, *Community Policing Defined* (Washington, DC: U.S. Department of Justice, Office of Community Oriented Policing Services, 2014).

[19] Ford, "Building Capability."

is key because they are able to make the decision to move forward and challenge the status quo by envisioning a different future for the police department and developing strategies and plans to achieve that vision.[20]

Adopting a COP ethos means that officers need to be empowered—and then trusted—to address a wide variety of situations. New ways of measuring an officer's performance and policies that value the prevention dimension of policing are necessary. Typically, police officers who perform well in responding to crimes or who arrest large numbers of criminals are rewarded or promoted, even when the legitimacy or legality of the means they use to apprehend criminals is under question. There is often too little recognition of officers who prevent crimes from occurring in the first place. COP institutions reduce reliance on a top-down approach and delegate authority and discretion, giving officers room to find creative solutions to community problems.[21] In COP, police officers must have the ability to make decisions and address problems innovatively.

The adoption of the COP ethos also calls for changes in the police academy training program. Training requirements must go beyond using firearms, driving, unarmed defense, and criminal law and procedures. Solving problems and establishing and maintaining partnerships with community members require skills such as de-escalation techniques; an understanding of human behavior, psychology, and the root causes of crime and violence; and an appreciation of cultural diversity and sensitivity. Police officers should be trained to handle most situations that arise in the community, to display good judgement, and to make the best decisions at any given moment. Police officers who are trained only to take orders and implement policies face difficulties in making sound judgements in the line of duty.

The institutional transformation that the adoption of COP requires is called for in recruitment policies as well. Recruitment policies can go a long way toward improving police diversity and should reflect the demographic composition of the population by focusing on the recruitment of minority officers. Adopting a community-oriented ethos requires reordering priorities and changes at the policy, planning, and operational levels.

---

[20] Ibid.
[21] Lawrence and McCarthy, "What Works in Community Policing?"

Impact of COP on Violent Extremism

An integrated COP approach allows police, in tandem with the community, to address social issues such as marginalization and discrimination. If left unaddressed, such issues may become grievances that could lead to RLVE or encourage and justify violence. Engagement of the police from a problem-solving perspective provides an opportunity to inform the community about services that the police and other government institutions provide. When police who focus on prevention and problem solving become aware of the potential risk factors of radicalization, they can act as the first respondents that they are supposed to be, thereby rendering justifications for violence against the police or any government institution or its population less valid. This proactive approach addresses both macro-level push and pull factors as well as the individual factors that may contribute to RLVE, and is thus an important component of increasing the resilience of communities.

Conclusion

The COP ethos promotes collaboration between police and communities to solve problems that threaten public safety. Community trust in the police increases, allowing community members to work more closely with police to build resilience against extremism and identify visible threats to public safety. Adopting the COP ethos involves changing not only the approach of the police, but also the way that police officers engage the community. It calls for profound change in the values and structure of the police force, creating an environment within which problem-solving techniques can be taught and sustainable and objective partnerships can be built.

CHAPTER 4

CHALLENGES IN ADOPTING COP

For many police institutions, adopting a COP ethos requires making significant changes in policies and practices in order to change the mindset and behavior of the entire police service. Resistance to such transformation may occur depending on officer and leadership perspectives. Police officers who support change will be interested in learning new skills and attending trainings. However, officers who believe that the current ways in which they operate are fair and adequate may express disdain and be reluctant to adopt new standards. This chapter discusses the potential pushback on and anticipated challenges to incorporating a COP ethos both within the police organization and among individual police officers.

Institutional Challenges

A police institution that is largely centralized and hierarchical with few individuals in positions of authority is incompatible with the spirit of COP.[1] In hierarchical police institutions, police officers have very little decision-making authority and can take limited actions without approval of the chief. This approach can severely impair proactive outreach to the community.

---

[1] Gerasimos A. Gianakis and G. John Davis, "Reinventing or Repackaging Public Services? The Case of Community-Oriented Policing," *Public Administration Review* 58, no. 6 (1998): 485–498.

COP calls for police officers to have autonomy in identifying problems and developing solutions as a situation evolves.[2] There are many situations where police officers need to make decisions without necessarily waiting for decisions to be made remotely or from the central command station. A centralized hierarchy is a structural impediment to public participation and could hinder implementation of COP.

Police institutions interested in a community orientation need to reorganize to maximize the agility of police as they respond to citizens and build a network with the community. A rigid chain of command is less conducive to the exchange of ideas and hinders a smooth flow of information, discouraging police officers from being problem solvers with analytical skills, skills that are necessary to approach and interact with communities and solve problems.

In many police departments, senior and midlevel officers are not graduates of the police academy but of the military academy. For example, since the establishment in 1956 of the Public Security Directorate in Jordan, only three out of twenty-seven directors (the institution's highest-ranking officer) have undergone basic police training; the rest have been former military commanders.[3] The nature of military training and the military's decision-making process means police officers are unlikely to be connected to and enjoy a sense of belonging within the community they serve.

In many countries, law enforcement is part of the national security establishment, and there is sometimes tension between the agenda of COP and national security. Police in many countries are expected to conduct robust operations, collect intelligence, use body armor, carry heavy military guns and equipment, and apply a zero-tolerance policy in the attempt to counter violent extremism. Many national security actors regard the burgeoning of the terrorism threat as a downfall for COP; some police have lost sight of their essential role of serving citizens and

---

[2] Herman Goldstein, *Problem-Oriented Policing* (New York: McGraw-Hill, 2015).

[3] Sarah Lyons-Padilla, Michele J. Gelfand, Hedieh Mirahmadi, Mehreen Farooq, and Marieke van Egmond, "Belonging Nowhere: Marginalization and Radicalization Risk among Muslim Immigrants," *Behavioral Science and Policy* 1, no. 2 (December 2015), 1–12.

protecting their rights, finding themselves entrenched in the national security agenda to defend against the new threat.[4]

Individual Challenges

The success of adopting a COP ethos depends on police officers implementing that ethos throughout all their activities.[5] However, obtaining police officer buy-in can be difficult. In some cases, "community policing" are just buzzwords that police departments use to improve their image in the eyes of the community without actually changing the behavior of police officers.[6] The lack of understanding of the COP ethos is a basic challenge to buy-in.

COP is often perceived as a vague and ill-defined concept.[7] Many police officers view community policing as an expression of an officer's personality, involving nothing more than being friendly to the citizenry and avoiding the use of unnecessary force. Others fear becoming de facto social workers or see COP as a philosophy that is imposed by police leadership interested in their own personal advancement.[8] COP is sometimes perceived by police officers as a way of describing what is already being practiced. Some officers see their jobs as being about responding to an individual incidents, and leave the task of solving underlying problems to other agencies and individuals.[9]

---

[4] Malcolm K. Sparrow, *Handcuffed: What Holds Policing Back, and the Keys to Reform* (Washington, DC: Brookings Institution Press, 2016).

[5] Arthur J. Lurigio and Wesley G. Skogan, "Winning the Hearts and Minds of Police Officers: An Assessment of Staff Perceptions of Community Policing in Chicago," *Crime and Delinquency* 40, no. 3 (July 1994): 315–330.

[6] Debra R. Cohen McCullough and Deborah L. Spence, *American Policing in 2022: Essays on the Future of a Profession* (Washington, DC: U.S. Department of Justice Office of Community Oriented Policing Services, September 2012).

[7] Ibid.

[8] Lori A. Cooke-Scott, "Community Based Policing in Ontario: Lessons from the Halton Regional Police Service," *Canadian Public Administration/Administration Publique Du Canada* 41, no. 1 (1998): 120–146.

[9] Adrian Leigh et al., "Problem-Oriented Policing: Brit Pop," in *Problem-Oriented Policing: Brit Pop* (London: Home Office, Police Policy Directorate, 1996).

Even when officers acquire an accurate understanding of COP and its potential to establish closer ties to the community, some officers will favor the change because they believe it will present opportunities to recruit informants, and are oblivious to the long-term problems that such a short-sighted attitude will create. Indeed, intelligence gathering that involves identifying at-risk youth often leads to traditional law enforcement rather than to problem-solving approaches that could help young people by engaging them in the community through employment or other positive contribution to their community.

Officers often have doubts about the notion of community empowerment and its use in policing. Some might not understand the value of getting information from the community about noncriminal activities. Others might feel that community engagement will dilute their ability to fight crime and terrorism if they get bogged down with additional work. Still others may feel that change implicitly means their current performance is substandard and may result in identifying the weaknesses of the policy rather than the benefits.[10]

The successful implementation of COP requires officers who are skilled at problem solving, decision making, communication, and technology.[11] Without an emphasis on these areas, as well as training on creative thinking, de-escalation, and cultural appreciation, police officers may not have the ability to operate in an environment that supports the COP ethos.

The policing culture has historically resisted innovation, including new approaches and methodologies such as community policing.[12] This resistance manifests itself in the priority accorded to officers' personal safety—another challenge to adopting COP. Police culture has been

---

[10] Richard Myers, "What Future(s) Do We Want for Community Policing?," in *Community Policing: The Past, Present, and Future* ed. Lorie Fridell and Mary Ann Wycoff (Police Executive Research Forum, Washington, DC; Annie E. Casey Foundation, Baltimore, MD, 2004), 169–182.

[11] Chang-Hun Lee and Chang-Bae Lee, "Factors Affecting Strategy Commitment to Community-Oriented Policing (COP) Among South Korean Police Officers," *Policing: An International Journal of Police Strategies and Management* 34, no. 4 (November 2011): 713–734.

[12] Steve Darroch and Lorraine Mazerolle, "Intelligence-Led Policing: A Comparative Analysis of Organizational Factors Influencing Innovation," *Police Quarterly* 16, no. 1 (November 19, 2012): 3–37.

oriented around the concept of identifying and responding to immediate threats and crimes within a community. This culture has led to overly aggressive responses to both real and perceived risks, and police officers often feel as though there are threats to their safety around every corner. This orientation has also prioritized the relationship between police partners, emphasizing the need to support and protect one's partner. However, this outlook can have the unintended effect of encouraging officers to support their colleagues even if their integrity may be compromised in doing so. Police services are often referred to through a familial lens, with officers described as brothers- or sisters-in-arms. Although this level of camaraderie is understandable given the physical dangers that certainly do exist and the extensive time an officer spends in his or her partner's company, this culture fosters an us-versus-them outlook toward citizens and further isolates police from the community.

The behavior and mindset of officers are by no means the only challenges to the adoption and implementation of a community-oriented ethos. COP requires organizational change—the most comprehensive and challenging type of change to effect. But if police leadership understand the process of change and how and why people resist change, they can design a process that minimizes or addresses resistance.[13] To achieve organizational transformation, leaders should first identify the underlying problem that they are attempting to resolve before discussing how a community-oriented police service will address the community concerns.

In adapting the COP ethos, leaders must create a sense of urgency.[14] Building a team to implement and oversee the process may help make the change more manageable and palatable for the entire police service. A working group of individuals who come from different parts of the police organization and have different knowledge and skills to help problem solve may be able to address this challenge.

---

[13] John P. Kotter, *Leading Change* (Boston: Harvard Business Review Press, 1996).
[14] Ibid.

Conclusion

The adoption of COP faces both institutional- and individual-level challenges because it requires complex and sensitive changes at strategic and operational levels. COP challenges traditional notions of the identity of police. A reliance on deterrence and coercion, combined with the threat of the use of force, may help enforce the rule of law but fail to facilitate respect for it. In today's complex security environment, the police need to reestablish respect for the rule of law. The professionalization of the police institution makes it more likely that communities will perceive the police as a service that is desirable and reliable and bolsters a community's welfare. Police institutions that opt to go through this type of transformation must include new policies and procedures and institute new training. The remainder of this book offers insights on training issues that need to be addressed to effectively adopt a COP ethos through the entire police organization.

PART II

THE CURRENT POLICE TRAINING CURRICULUM

CHAPTER 5
A TYPICAL TRAINING PROGRAM

Training is a crucial tool for facilitating change within any organization. To successfully implement COP, training programs must reflect the changes recommended for police departments.[1] Multiple studies indicate that a direct relationship exists between the training recruits receive in police academies and the behavior they demonstrate to the public.[2] As police institutions move towards COP, supplementary training and education will become increasingly important. Before introducing such supplementary programs, however, it is helpful to assess the existing state of instruction in order to understand how best to augment what is currently being delivered.

Many police departments claim to have adopted a COP approach and problem-oriented policing practices. Yet a review of current training curricula indicates that many police academies continue to function as hierarchical and militaristic organizations.[3] The typical training program is focused on tactical techniques—such as the use of force and first aid—

---

[1] Michael L. Birzer, "The Theory of Andragogy Applied to Police Training," *Policing: An International Journal of Police Strategies and Management* 26, no. 1 (2003): 29–42.

[2] Olga Bykov, "Police Academy Training: An Evaluation of the Strengths and Weaknesses of Police Academies," *Themis: Research Journal of Justice Studies and Forensic Science* 2, no. 1 (2014): 142–159.

[3] Allison T. Chappell and Lonn Lanza-Kaduce, "Police Academy Socialization: Understanding the Lessons Learned in a Paramilitary-Bureaucratic Organization," *Journal of Contemporary Ethnography* 39, no. 2 (December 29, 2009): 187–214.

rather than on skills related to community- and problem-oriented policing. No international standardized content or length of training exists, and there is no agreement about the perfect curriculum that will produce an effective and professional police officer. In each organization, the leadership determines the content of the training curriculum.

This chapter provides an overview of typical training in police academies and sheds light on the key messages that police officers absorb as a result of their training (which typically encompasses 450 to 600 training hours). The analysis discusses the two kinds of training recruits that receive: knowledge-based instruction and training in practical skills. The chapter suggests that, in its current form, police academy training does not adequately prepare officers to perform tasks related to their duties. The overview presented here is based on curricula in various countries in Africa, the Middle East, and the Balkans.

Core Courses: Knowledge-Based

Typically, the curriculum of a police academy includes the following knowledge-based subjects.

Introduction to Law Enforcement

This topic is most often the initial module of a program and aims to socialize recruits in the mores of the law enforcement environment and to introduce terminology. Content includes the local history of the police force and the evolution of local law enforcement since its establishment. During this introduction, recruits learn about the organizational structure, the concept of and respect for the chain of command, and the core values of the organization, including, but not limited to, integrity, high-quality service provision, accountability, and cooperation. Recruits are introduced to the administrative, logistical, and financial departments in the police organization. The main roles and responsibilities of law enforcement officers in society are also discussed. The role of police in protecting individual rights, prevention versus intervention techniques, and community and government expectations of law enforcement officers are introduced.

Introduction to the Criminal Justice System

This section of training introduces police officers to the structure of the criminal justice system in their country. The main actors in the criminal justice system—including but not limited to prosecutors, judges, and corrections agencies—are identified. During this portion of training, recruits are introduced to the components of criminal justice, including the court and trial process, prosecution, defense attorneys, correction/detention centers, and how the criminal justice system works. This overview allows officers to better understand that police are just one element within the larger criminal justice system. Upon completion of this module, recruits are able to identify the roles and responsibilities of police officers and understand how police officers differ from and support other actors within the criminal justice system.

Legislative Training

This section of training considers the legal basis for police authority and action such as arrest, use of force, and search and seizure, as well as the limits on law enforcement activity.

Criminal Law. Classifications of criminal offences are discussed in addition to how different crimes are categorized in the legal sense and what the penalties for crimes may be. Upon completion of training, recruits are able to identify crimes against persons—such as murder and physical or sexual assault and abuse—versus crimes against property—such as burglary, theft, and damage to property. Recruits also learn the elements that constitute each crime. Recruits are introduced to procedural law to better understand how a crime plays out from the police's initial arrival at a scene to the trial process and through to the possibility of conviction.

Constitutional Law. This segment of training discusses the relationship between different entities within a state, namely, the executive, legislature, and judiciary branches. Recruits are introduced to the main articles of the constitution that refer to the rights of the citizen.

Juvenile Law. This module teaches recruits about the juvenile code (including the national definition of juvenile), legal issues as they pertain to young people, the appropriate procedures for an encounter with juveniles, and the police and court authorities who handle juvenile delinquency and criminal problems.

Human Rights Law: Recruits are provided with an overview of the Universal Declaration of Human Rights as well as international conventions as they relate to women and children, if these documents have been recognized by their country. Recruits learn that everyone has equal protection under the law, without discrimination on any grounds. Officers are taught about the appropriate methods to use if they want to arrest someone. Limitation of use of force and detainees' rights, including the right to legal representation and to notify a relative of arrest, are typically covered.

Traffic Law. Recruits become familiar with their country's traffic laws and ordinances, including those related to operator licensing, vehicle registration, insurance and equipment requirements, and how to read road traffic signs, as well as what constitutes a minor versus a major traffic offense. Recruits learn how to fill out paper citations and control street traffic.

Use of Force Requirements. Recruits are introduced to the legal guidance on the use of force, and to principles of use of force such as proportionality and the continuum of force; where included, recruits are taught to use no more force than necessary to subdue a suspect.[4] By emphasizing the personal safety of an officer and introducing less lethal options as alternatives to force, recruits are expected to identify the situations in which the use of force is legitimate. Recruits are also taught to define and give examples of unlawful force, excessive use of force, force continuum, and levels of resistance from a suspect.

---

[4] Nancy Marion, "Police Academy Training: Are We Teaching Recruits What They Need to Know?," *Policing: An International Journal of Police Strategies & Management* 21, no. 1 (1998): 54–79.

Other Training Topics

Customer Service. This module aims to improve police officers' general communication skills to enhance the quality of their interactions with citizens, including the way in which police communicate with those with whom they come into contact when they conduct street/traffic stops, respond to victims of crime, and respond to calls for service.

Criminal Investigation. This section of the training aims to equip recruits with interviewing and investigation skills so that they are able to take statements and question suspects. During this module, recruits learn how to protect a crime scene from contamination as a first responder. They also learn about search and seizure procedures in addition to how to prepare search warrants. They are also taught how to protect a crime scene and how to take crime scene notes and otherwise document the scene.

Community Policing. During this module, recruits learn about the relevance of community-police partnership. Topics such as respect for diversity and police bias are taught to equip officers with tools to demonstrate respect for the public and to foster a collaborative relationship with the public. This module typically lasts only four to six hours.

Stress Management. Recruits are provided with lessons on resilience and stress management to increase their ability to adapt to a myriad of professional situations and cope with high levels of pressure. This training aims to help officers manage their anger and emotions effectively. Recruits are introduced to a general understanding of the causes of stress and presented with healthy, appropriate coping mechanisms.

Code of Conduct. Current training aims to promote the efficiency of police officers by teaching them to obey a code of conduct and the rules and procedures of the police department or face disciplinary action for violating them. This training also aims to prevent misconduct from happening and to enhance an officer's professionalism. Agency policies, rules and regulations, and definitions of minor and major misconduct are covered in this module. Recruits are taught about the effect of misconduct on their careers and their potential for promotion as well as the role and duties of internal affairs in investigating potential infractions.

Tactical Training: Skills-Based

The skills-based aspects of a police academy curriculum include the following.

Weapons Training

This section of training aims to equip the recruit with the knowledge, competence, and confidence to carry and use diverse types of weapons effectively. Recruits learn how to assemble and disassemble weapons and fire, load, unload, and clean multiple types of guns, including automatic weaponry. They learn different shooting positions and the advantages and disadvantages of each position, in addition to firearms safety. During this training, recruits experience several realistic firearms scenarios designed to instill confidence and prepare them for the experience of firing their weapon in the field. The importance of writing a report immediately after a shooting incident is highlighted.

Defensive Tactics

Recruits are taught self-defense techniques and nonlethal suspect control methods, such as how to engage in one-on-one combat using karate or tai-kwon do techniques. Recruits learn procedures for making an arrest, including appropriate handcuffing procedures, as well as how to respond to those resisting arrest.

Driving Skills

Recruits learn defensive driving techniques, how to stay aware of road conditions, emergency vehicle operation (including siren protocol), and emergency driving in pursuit situations, as well as how to respond to traffic accidents.

First Aid

Recruits learn how to perform an initial medical assessment of injured people and how to provide first aid treatment, including how to apply a tourniquet, how to care for unconscious casualties, bandaging wounds and bleeding, and caring for burns and heart conditions. During this module, accident reporting is covered so recruits are aware of the appropriate information to capture depending on a situation.

Radio and Communication

This training familiarizes recruits with the use of radio equipment and appropriate radio procedures, message transmission and call signs, and encryption.

Physical Fitness

Physical fitness sessions include stretching, running, pushups, speed, and agility.

Drilling and Marching

Recruits learn how to execute basic movements such as attention and salute and how to respond to other vocal commands. Recruits learn military protocol for saluting the flag and marching in unison.

The Limitations of the Typical Approach

Recruits go through an intense basic training, both in the classroom and in the field. The curriculum lasts twelve to eighteen weeks and prepares recruits for employment as well as providing them with professional socialization.[5] Training shapes the expected physical and mental characteristics of police officers and equips them with skills to serve and protect their community. However, instructors tend to exaggerate select elements of the training,

---

[5] Daniel M. Blumberg et al., "Impact of Police Academy Training on Recruits' Integrity," *Police Quarterly* 19, no. 1 (March 1, 2015): 63–86.

which can create problems for the recruits when they put their training into practice as full-fledged officers. For example, one curriculum that was reviewed overemphasized the legal and physical aspects of policing as opposed to administrative training, and thus topics such as procedures and practices around filling complaints, misconduct, ethics, and diversity received little attention.

Typical police training programs seek to generate two learning outcomes, namely, the acquisition of knowledge and the acquisition of skills. The cognitive component is mostly taught in the classroom and is instruction based; as described above, classes cover subjects such as an introduction to the police and criminal justice system, the laws of the country, and police policies and rules. Some of the tactical training may also be delivered in the classroom, where recruits may be taught about topics such as the use of weapons, officer safety, use of force, and first aid.

Although the material that is covered is necessary, the ways in which it is taught may deter recruits from retaining the information they are given. The amount covered is normally vast; recruits are responsible for reading and retaining information from many books and handouts. Recruits may be overwhelmed by the need to memorize large amounts of material in a short period while being continuously reminded of the need to achieve a high grade. The training program is especially challenging for those who have difficulty reading and writing and those who have been out of school for extended periods of time.

The curriculum often contains a significant gap: recruits are not taught how all the material they must retain is applicable to the daily work of an officer. Although it is sometimes implied, a direct connection is rarely made. For example, teaching a recruit about human rights does not mean that person will necessarily respect citizens' rights when patrolling the streets. Police officers need to learn about policies and best practices that deconstruct the concepts of human rights to transform knowledge into practical behavior that will help them to avoid violations of human rights, such as illegal search and seizure and excessive use of force.

Information is usually imparted in the classroom via traditional lecturing, with little to no interaction between the instructor and the audience. The lack of the practical exercises and scenarios may make recruits less interested in listening to the material at hand, and they often attempt to shift topics to more exciting stories from the field.

There is a direct relationship between the training that recruits receive in the academy and the attitudes they hold about policing. The culture encouraged by a paramilitary approach to police training may produce officers with an uncompromising mindset. The training environment is separate from the broader community, and the focus of the curriculum is on rules and strict obedience rather than on serving the needs of the people. To implement a COP ethos, police officers should be trained to have the ability to earn the respect of the public and to understand that, if they do not earn it, they are likely to find the community unwilling to provide assistance.

The typical police academy program provides residences for the recruits, meaning that recruits live together for most of their training period. The rationale behind this is that recruits will be socialized to the police environment quickly through this immersion process. However, this environment may place undue stress on recruits, who are forced to follow elaborate and rigid rules and regulations. Mandatory on-site residence may limit recruitment efforts.

Recruits may be subject to physical discipline, additional work assignments, or verbal harassment as punishment for failing to follow procedures. In some cases, stress is deliberately placed on recruits by trainers to determine how they will handle it in the field. Recruits are told to memorize what they have been taught and quizzed daily in an effort to develop discipline.

Typical training pays little to no attention to the COP ethos. A COP ethos is based on partnering and communicating with the public and should be integrated into all components of a police training program. Currently, if academies teach recruits anything about community policing, they devote only a few hours to the subject.

Conclusion

A review of current police academy training indicates that gaps exist and that training modules, as they are currently taught, do not necessarily meet the educational and training objectives of a COP service. Police academies need to shift toward a more thorough curriculum that has a greater focus on skills and higher expectations for graduation; inadequate preparation of police recruits will set new officers up for failure. Modules should address the root causes of crime to include violent extremism, human behavior, and problem-solving and communication skills. These courses could be taught in lieu of topics such as infantry training, with less time spent on modules such as weapons training and defensive tactics. Police academies should strive to produce skilled officers who know how to protect and serve the community and are able to empower those around them to peacefully resolve their own problems. In sum, training of recruits should be restructured to provide an in-depth understanding of the role of the police in the community. The following chapter elaborates on these suggestions.

CHAPTER 6

IMPACT OF THE CURRENT TRAINING PROGRAM

International experts disagree about how police academy training programs should be designed and what outcomes they should aim to generate, but there is no disagreement about the powerful and enduring influence that academies exert.[1] The academy shapes the characteristics of the police service and equips officers with certain skills. The content, methodology, and mindset that underpin officer training influence the actions and behavior that officers display every day on duty. That behavior has a direct impact on the confidence of the community in the police. To adopt a COP ethos, the academy must reconsider the outcomes of training to determine how it impacts both the officer and the community.

This chapter analyzes the impact of a training program on the conduct of police officers, focusing on their reputation and credibility in the community. It identifies opportunities for enhancing the current program with knowledge- or skills-based training. Without the addition of COP-relevant content, training will negatively impact the behavior of police officers as well as impair their relationship with the community, undercutting their ability to be made aware of problems that may fuel larger grievances and fester into violent extremism.

---

[1] Michael D. White, "Identifying Good Cops Early: Predicting Recruit Performance in the Academy," *Police Quarterly* 11, no. 1 (March 1, 2008): 27–49.

Effect of Current Training on Police Behavior

A Heavy-Handed Approach

The nature of police training can shift the mindset of a recruit toward a heavy-handed approach to law enforcement and crime prevention. Marching, drilling, and an overemphasis on shooting and defensive tactics, areas that consume a large share of current training, send a message to the recruits that they live in a hostile world where they must fight to survive. This message is also imparted by an overemphasis on officer safety. Recruits are consistently reminded that risk is everywhere and that they should assume that anyone is capable of extraordinary violence.

Recruits are discouraged from questioning authority and are taught to respect and carry out orders without argument or question. The training environment, which is often physically separated from the broader community, denies officers the opportunity to interact with individuals not in the police force.

The current curriculum focuses on rules and obedience rather than on serving the needs of people. This method of teaching and training is likely to produce an authoritarian mentality: police officers who value the effect of punishment and rely on the authority vested in their uniform to gain compliance from those with whom they interact. For example, police officers often use rough, stern language and behave in a rude manner, behavior that is modeled from the top down in the academy. The tone of training reinforces a police culture that is centered on traditional law enforcement practices, which can fuel community grievances and enhance the appeal of violent extremist messages.

A police department considering adopting a COP approach will need to effect a significant shift in training and culture. Officers tend to perceive members of the community as people to be policed, rather than as people to police alongside. Upon completion of basic training, some recruits will express negativity toward their community, viewing it as a source of danger and a threat to the officers' safety.[2] This perspective can lead to viewing those who are active or outspoken in the community as criminal and blur

---

[2] Stoughton, "Law Enforcement's 'Warrior' Problem."

the line in officers' minds between terrorists and criminals, on the one side, and an active and engaged citizenry, on the other.

Lack of Problem-Solving Skills

Police spend vast amounts of time responding to issues not necessarily criminal in nature.[3] However, an analysis of basic training curriculum reveals that problem-solving and interpersonal skills are a low priority. Basic training does not teach police officers how to communicate or reason with people to manage a wide range of situations. Four hours of training under the heading of "Community Policing" are not enough to learn the essential communication techniques that allow officers to resolve conflicts effectively. It is not surprising that officers are often uncertain as to whether they are responding to a call in an appropriate way.

For example, when responding to a routine traffic accident, an officer needs to determine if the victim wants to press charges. If the victim decides not to pursue legal action, the parties may look for an alternative way to resolve the situation. An officer who has undergone typical training may not be able to offer them much help. But if the officer has been trained to address conflict, or potential conflict, with a problem-solving approach, he or she will look for a win-win outcome and may be able to propose a solution that is acceptable to both parties. Such an approach will not only avoid conflict but also boost the legitimacy of the police officer as a service provider, which is the goal of the COP ethos. That same approach, with its concern to solve problems peacefully rather than generate grievances, is obviously relevant to CVE.

Training needs to be adapted to include ways to emphasize the ability of officers to address the many calls for service that require interpersonal skills. As a result of strengthening the curriculum, police will feel more confident in their ability to de-escalate conflict and thus avoid violence.

---

[3] Allison T. Chappell, "Police Academy Training: Comparing Across Curricula," *Policing: An International Journal of Police Strategies & Management* 31, no. 1 (August 29, 2007): 36–56.

Lack of Discretion to Make Decisions

Officers need autonomy to do their job. However, giving an officer discretionary power without the appropriate education and training may lead to undesirable consequences and to abuses of that power. Officers need the critical thinking skills to enable them to exercise their authority wisely. Station commanders may try to minimize this autonomy, as they may not believe that officers have the capability to respond to and solve the underlying problem in a given situation. For this reason, they may require officers to run all decisions past them before proceeding. This step can be time consuming and labor intensive, requiring additional reports and follow-up.

For community members who may not be privy to this process, it may be interpreted as unnecessarily bureaucratic and time consuming, delaying their desire for justice. By strengthening the knowledge and skills of officers within the academy, the trust from commanders in the decision-making authority of officers will increase.

Poor Community Collaboration

Recruits are told from the first day of training that their primary duty is to enforce the law and that the core mission of the police is to control crime. When only enforcement and crime control are emphasized, officers graduate without an understanding about how to work with the community. Yet, the mission of the police cannot be achieved without true collaboration with the community. Community trust, confidence, and participation are vital to mission achievement.[4] Police need to understand that effective policing hinges on citizens actively contributing to violence and crime prevention by sharing information they may have and calling the policing when threats arise. For example, if there is an increased rate of car thefts in a neighborhood, community members should have access to information about what is happening. Without community support and situational understanding, officers find it harder to solve problems. By

---

[4] Kevin Mark Dunn et al., "Can You Use Community Policing for Counter Terrorism? Evidence from NSW, Australia," *Police Practice and Research* 17, no. 3 (2015): 196–211.

working together, the police and the community mutually benefit, with as citizens and their property enjoying police protection while officers are better placed to deter criminal behavior.

It should be noted that a significant level of trust and confidence in police is needed for this type of collaboration to happen in RLVE cases, because parents or siblings have to trust the police to handle suspicious behavior effectively, without using violence, and within the legal framework.

Effect of Current Training on the Community

Mistrust of the Police Force

Mistrust between police officers and the community can be seen as a direct consequence of current training. The use of force is presented as the easiest way to solve problems. However, most calls to police are made by people hoping to resolve situations or in search of social services; reporting incidents that are not directly criminal in nature; or notifying police about incidents where there is no need to use force. A professional police officer with a suite of skills and the ability to offer solutions, who can exercise good judgment when resolving conflicts and solving problems rather than escalating the situation, is called for.[5]

Police officers who lack restraint in the face of violence or the threat of it and who have not been taught de-escalation skills will not have the tools to handle tense situations without resorting to the use of force. They may rush to use force to solve issues rather than considering more appropriate courses of action, such as withdrawing from the scene or refraining from making an arrest until backup support arrives.

Community often do not trust police to solve their problems and may not consider the police a safe, effective recourse. In addition, excessive use of force by police in the past make people fear them. Although nothing can reverse history, the past use of violence may be addressed going forward through a comprehensive, locally relevant training focused on the needs of the community and the police force.

---

[5] Samuel Walker and Charles M. Katz, *The Police in America: An Introduction*, 6th ed. (New York: McGraw-Hill Education, 2007).

Typical training does not empower officers to respond to people who are physically or mentally ill or disabled. Because they may have experienced a lack of understanding in past encounters with the police, those suffering from a disability may not feel as though they can trust the police to respond appropriately when assistance is required. In addition, police officers may perceive erratic behavior as threatening and respond with force. Some individuals and their families may have developed a fear of the police and exhibit paranoia in the presence of police officers, which may be misinterpreted as suspicious behavior by those officers. The interactions between police and those suffering from a mental or emotional illness can end fatally without adequate officer education and training.[6]

Little Respect for Diverse Communities

Topics such as respect for cultural, religious or political differences, unintended or implicit racial bias, and prejudices are more often than not omitted from police academy curricula Little to no attention is paid to diversity training and appreciation for diversity. Without directly addressing preexisting biases and understanding how to communicate across cultural, ideological, religious, and identity barriers, officers may misread a situation and see a threat where none actually exists. Better training on these topics and a deeper understanding of networks and communities that exist within a society may help officers see different options when they respond to requests.

One step to reduce the biases of police officers is to train them about fair and impartial policing and how to recognize and mitigate their own biases. Training with a focus on fair and impartial treatment of offenders is crucial. Biases are often based on one's view of "the other," centering on such factors as gender, sexual orientation, political affiliations, race, or religion. Training should aim to show police officers how to recognize and manage their biases so that they will not impact or influence the officers' professional decisions. This training should also equip police officers with tools to demonstrate a respect for the public regardless of the age, sex, race, or religion of any person and to eliminate the use of violent and

---

[6] Farzana B. Kara, "Police Interactions with the Mentally Ill: The Role of Procedural Justice," *Canadian Graduate Journal of Sociology and Criminology* 3, no. 1 (2014): 79.

excessive force. Lack of training on identity, especially for police officers who have had few positive interactions with diverse communities in the past, will lead to misinterpretations and misunderstandings of the behavior of specific populations in their communities, which might widen cleavages between police and communities.

Different Perceptions of the Role of the Police

Recruits are taught that a positive evaluation of an officer's performance by police leadership is based on obedience to orders and high rates of arrest, ticket issuance, and criminal convictions. This data-driven approach is what police use as a parameter that determines safe and secure communities. With that in mind, police normally deploy personnel in areas that have high crime rates with the assumption that increased police presence and heightened police intervention will decrease crime over time while also ensuring that departmental monthly quotas are met. This approach does not take into consideration the damage it causes in many communities. It does not display an understanding of what people want, and instead accentuates the schism between the police and the community.

Civilians do not measure the safety and security of their environment solely by the absence of crimes; for most citizens, fair enforcement of the law is also a key metric. For example, if police stop and search a hundred individuals looking for weapons and find two, then—according to the police—they have succeeded in taking two weapons off the street. However, from the perspective of the community, ninety-eight individuals were bothered unnecessarily by the police.

The Inadequacy of Current Training on Police Capacity for CVE

Ideally, law enforcement personnel are trained to contribute to prevention policies and strategies to counter violent extremism. Officers must know how to identify potential signs of radicalization, determine initial indicators of a potential threat, mitigate their role as drivers of violent extremism, and support individuals who may be vulnerable to radicalization. However, in reviewing the current police training, it is clear that police officers are not trained to understand the threat of violent extremism and its drivers, hate crimes, hate groups, political crimes, the RLVE process, or types of CVE interventions. Thus, the police force is not well prepared to prevent or respond to the threat posed by violent extremism. It is uncommon to see a police service that is willing to dig into a situation in order to identify the root causes of violent extremism. Officers are rarely given the opportunity to be concerned about preventing actions; instead, they respond to criminal activity and arrest perpetrators.

Periodic lectures are given to recruits during basic training to increase their awareness of violent extremist threats. However, most of those lectures emphasize the concept that religiously-based violent extremists pose the most significant threat to national security and public safety. Such lectures should make clear that threats can come from other violent extremist organizations, too- such as politically-based violent extremist organizations- and thus give recruits a keener understanding of the nature and variety of violent extremism. Furthermore, recruits should be taught to differentiate between groups such as revolutionaries, nationalists, minority separatists, and reformists to ensure that those who question the status quo are not automatically seen as violent extremists.

Recruits normally receive training on the protection of critical infrastructures and official facilities, ministries, and houses of high officials. They thus may interpret threats as threats to physical structures or the lives within them, not as threats to the minds and the hearts of people.

Understanding the root causes of violent extremism is crucial for officers, who must be aware of their ability to mitigate the likelihood of RLVE. Without deep understanding of the root causes of crime and violence, officers run the risk of grouping all criminals in the same category and ignoring the social nuances of the community in which they operate. By including training on root causes, the academy would highlight the importance of understanding one's community and help officers to recognize that they have potential ways to disrupt the radicalization process. For example, if young people are being arrested for committing petty crimes due to a lack of adult supervision and the availability of activities, an understanding of the situation could lead a police service to advocate for building a community recreation center to provide a safe, entertaining alternative to criminal activity. This alternate space could also provide a supervised arena for young people to meet new role models and be exposed to new ways of thinking, potentially creating a deterrent to the lure of radicalization.

Police should not be an arm of whatever political party has attained power within the government.[7] However, because current training places an emphasis on the protection of government and high-ranking officials, police officers often feel that they serve the interests of the politically powerful elite rather than the interests of the community. When a clash of interests is exposed between the community and the government, the police ultimately take the side of the government. This could create an opening for extremists to advance their arguments and recruit individuals who have been negatively impacted by police activities and an unstable environment. There is an inherent danger that police academy training will result in the strengthening of the perception that the police department is politicized or deployed to protect the status quo and quell dissident and/ or minority groups. A police academy program must reflect not only the government's strategic plan but also community interests and priorities.

Conclusion

In order to equip officers to pave the way for COP to be adopted, police departments must focus on the connection between performance in the academy and performance on the street. The solution to the challenge of better linking academy training to real-world policing involves the development of more practical and realistic academy training programs.[8] Police academies should seize the opportunity to revise their curricula to make it more related to the challenges faced by officers in their daily work. The next two parts of the book present training modules that, if they are incorporated into the current policing training curriculum, can teach officers how to better respond to the immediate and long-term needs of the community by adopting a COP ethos. Each module is described, its impact explained, and the consequences of *not* including it in the curriculum discussed.

---

[7] Clive Emsley, "The Birth and Development of the Police," in Ted Newburn, ed., *Handbook of Policing* 2nd ed. (New York: Taylor and Francis, 2008), 66–83.

[8] White, "Identifying Good Cops Early."

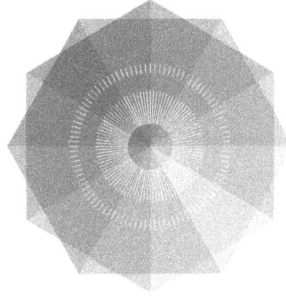

PART III

MODULES FOR COP: SHIFTING THE ATTITUDE AND BEHAVIOR OF POLICE INSTITUTIONS

CHAPTER 7

EARN PUBLIC CONFIDENCE

A police department's orientation towards the community must be shifted with a specific goal in mind—namely, gaining community confidence in the mission of the police. Such confidence underpins all components of COP. Effective training is a step toward attaining this lofty aspiration. Post-training, police can realize the benefits of community confidence through tangible actions. Community confidence is demonstrated through feedback from and actions taken by individual members of the community. This symbiotic relationship leads to effective CVE efforts. This chapter presents a knowledge-based module to develop police officers' capacity for CVE by collaborating with the community. It teaches police how to earn community confidence and how to capitalize on this confidence to counter violent extremism. This chapter outlines what academy cadets and serving officers need to know about the nature of public confidence in police.

Impact of Module's Inclusion

Public confidence is the source of a police service's strength and effectiveness. Police need public confidence to develop the capacity to address problems that lead to violent extremist activity. To win public confidence (and it does need to be *won*—there should be no doubt that it must be earned and never taken for granted), police must develop, maintain, and grow partnerships, collaboratively solve problems with communities, and change their organizational culture. Police must also shift their attitudes to a community-oriented, "police for others" mindset when dealing with the public both during routine daily activities and on emergency calls. Police must reform to earn the public's confidence, and they need this confidence to reform—the two are mutually reinforcing and underpin the police's capacity to embody a community-oriented ethos.

Because the police force is a prominent public face of the state, the legitimacy of the police and the wider government rests in part on the public's confidence in police and trust that these state agents do their jobs professionally. After learning about public confidence, police officers will better understand how their actions contribute to public perceptions of legitimacy. With respect to CVE, when the public sees police as legitimate, then they are more likely to cooperate and actively partner in policing violent extremism. As two scholars of criminology have observed, "Where authorities are judged to be legitimate, people feel that they ought to defer to their decisions and rules, cooperate with them and follow them voluntarily out of obligation rather than out of fear of punishment or anticipation of reward."[1]

A significant level of legitimacy is a precondition for successful proactive community outreach and for responding to calls for help. If police understand the importance of public confidence and how they can raise the level of confidence through their actions and behaviors, then they can increase the public's willingness to cooperate with police. This does not mean simply voluntary compliance with the law on the part of citizens, but also coming forward with problems. This module provides an understanding of what the public pays attention to when making judgements about confidence, giving police a basis for applying the skills outlined in part IV, particularly regarding creating partnerships.

Police officers need to understand what kind of behavior on their part is likely to make community members more willing to cooperate with the police and readier to come forward with information regarding community problems that may not be criminal in nature. Police availability

---

[1] Kristina Murphy and Adrian Cherney, "Understanding Cooperation with Police in a Diverse Society," *British Journal of Criminology* 52, no. 1 (August 19, 2011): 181–201.

and responsiveness contribute to the legitimacy of the police, and with greater legitimacy comes greater effectiveness.

This module will leave cadets with an increased awareness of how fairness, embodied operationally in procedural justice, buttresses public perceptions and expectations of the police and the wider government. Recruits will learn about the positive ramifications of treating people fairly, respectfully explaining why they are taking the actions they are, and giving the public an opportunity to respond. They will have a greater awareness of how their actions indicate to the public how the government sees them as individuals, always respectful of their background and identity.

Impact of Module's Omission

Without an understanding of the importance of public confidence in police and an understanding that police actions before, during, and after public encounters can enhance or break public confidence, police are likely to see their organization as the source of societal stability and the only option for preventing, responding to, and prosecuting crime. The uniform, training, language, dangerous nature of the job, equipment, and role in society all promote an insular, "police-against-others" worldview. To avoid this, police must fully understand why they should rely on the public and foster public conviction in police.

Without an understanding of the importance of the public partnership, police will have less awareness of how their actions influence public perceptions of police. They will be forced to use intuition to guess how the public gains and loses confidence in police. This can have a detrimental effect on voluntary compliance with the law and whether people share information. Without paying appropriate attention to why people in the community see police negatively or positively, local threats will spread. Police will not be able to effectively work with communities to be more cognizant of these threats and overcome other challenges. People may not obey police as often or as readily and could be less willing to call on them for help. Police and communities will be left to deal with threats such as violent extremism in isolation from one another or, even worse, will work at odds with each other. These unaddressed challenges and threats make officers, along with the communities they serve, less safe.

Another effect of not knowing how to build confidence might be an internal call for a stronger show of force before and after terrorist attacks. To enhance public confidence, police institutions often strive to increase funding, hardware, or other tangible and visible resources. Yet a focus on building the police in this way is based on the premise that police can rely only on themselves to prevent, respond to, and prosecute crime. Instead, as one specialist in international criminal justice, David Bayley, argues, the police need to be outward-looking: "To be truly effective ... the police [rely on] a public that would notify them of crime, identify likely suspects, undertake self-protection, and mobilize informal opinion against potential law-breakers."[2] When officers think that confidence is won by looking and acting "tough," they have less incentive to use knowledge and skills to build reputations as protectors of the communities they serve. Instead, they rely on force rather than earned confidence and moral authority to win the community's trust.

Themes of Instruction

The first of the following subsections discusses what exactly is meant by "confidence" and why it is important; the subsequent subsections explain how police actions affect it.

Define Public Confidence

First, one must acknowledge that confidence can seem like a vague concept. Confidence is a psychological state that exists in each person's mind; nonetheless, it can be measured. Although frontline officers and detectives are not expected to carry out large-scale surveys to determine public attitudes toward police and how they do their jobs, it is nevertheless important to emphasize that officers' actions have a direct impact on how individual members of the public see the police institution. Each individual officer has a direct effect on how everyone in the organization is perceived.

In this sense, public confidence is a broader concept than trust in

---

[2] David H. Bayley, "Police Reform: Who Done It?" *Policing and Society* 18, no. 1 (2008): 7–17.

police. Trust can be built between individuals and involves a component of faith. Confidence elevates the idea of trust to an ethos, where every person in the police organization seeks public confidence as a goal through every action he or she takes. The difference between trust and confidence is analogous to the difference between a piece of rope and a net. Like a piece of rope with two ends, a police officer assigned to a specific neighborhood is the connection between the police organization and the community. People may trust their officer but not necessarily the rest of the unit. Confidence, on the other hand, resides in a police organization where all members embody a COP ethos, and any member of society expects that whoever shows up wearing a uniform and badge will be available, respectful, responsive, and fair.

Both trust and confidence involve risk on the part of the public—the less powerful party. People's experiences, and those of community leaders, friends, and family members, reinforce their perception of the police and their expectations that police officers will do their job as they should, no matter what. This evidence base fosters confidence and takes blind faith out of the police-public relationship.

For CVE, because one police officer represents all police, the public needs to know that any person can come forward with information to any officer. This is a tangible manifestation of confidence in police, and it is a vital relationship for police to foster so they can identify grievances, social trends, and narratives. Members of the public need to know they can come forward with information about people who are potentially becoming radicalized or that are marginalized, especially because it is extremely difficult for police by themselves to discover such noncriminal trends without exacerbating them. Tom Tyler, an expert on issues of legitimacy, sums up the situation neatly: "If citizens do not trust the system, they will not use it."[3]

Police officers with this understanding of confidence will, at the individual level, understand how their actions contribute to how the community bases its judgments about the police. The ability to perceive why people do or do not comply with orders must be based on knowledge,

---

[3] Tyler, "Psychological Perspectives," 291.

and officers can temper their responses and use techniques to persuade compliance.

Public confidence in police lessens the need for police to take heavy-handed actions in response to terrorism. This is important because police use of force (while sometimes necessary) carries the risk of continuing a cycle of violence and generating new or additional grievances, which lessens public confidence. If the public is unwilling to cooperate with, or actively resists, police actions, then police are at risk. When police have a solid understanding of the components of public confidence, their legitimacy and thus their effectiveness and safety increases.[4]

Establish Legitimacy

Violent extremists are well aware that they cannot operate effectively without community support for or community acquiescence to their actions. To undercut the appeal of violent extremism, police must undercut this tacit or active support by proactively engaging and establishing their own legitimacy with the community However, police need to carefully consider how the community perceives them before attempting to engage. The rest of this chapter identifies various opportunities that police can take to should create to prevent violence and crime by earning legitimacy.

Foster Community Partnerships

To create strong partnerships in communities with the goal of enhancing CVE efforts, the police must first make efforts to understand community members and how they perceive police. One way to do this is by understanding existing violent extremist narratives and how and why they resonate.

Narratives are a powerful recruiting tool for violent extremists but can be equally influential in preventing radicalization. Police are a part of community narratives and exist in competition with violent extremists for legitimacy. But before police can alter their own narratives, through words

---

[4] David H. Bayley and Robert M. Perito, "The Police in War: Fighting Insurgency, Terrorism, and Violent Crime," in *The Police in War: Fighting Insurgency, Terrorism, and Violent Crime* (Boulder, CO: Lynne Rienner Publishers, 2010), 99.

and actions, it is important to understand how narratives are exploited and used by extremists. The master narratives of violent extremist organizations are critical to understanding the war of ideas that extremists use to define their culture and actions.[5]

Consider the narrative propagated by Islamic State, or ISIS. ISIS signals that it creates the ideal political entity, that is, "the Islamic state." This state differs from all others, which supporters characterize as full of injustice, oppression, and corruption. Many Muslims find this ideal very powerful, but it is little understood outside of these communities.[6] This ideal, combined with a general lack of public confidence in an existing government, can give credence to ISIS's promises to upend and replace the status quo. People are drawn to support this promised change.

For example, a young man named Kamal lives in Douar Hicher, a town outside of Tunisia's capital. He can be described as "on the fence." Prepared to support the most legitimate authority, he applied to join the police force, where many of his family members work, and was rejected. He found ISIS's call compelling because it symbolized the potential for "justice and peace." He called it "the project," implying that in supporting ISIS, he was taking agency over his life and proactively building a new, religiously sanctioned country. ISIS offered a preferable alternative to Tunisian authorities, whom he saw as "infidels" and lacking legitimacy.[7]

It is not enough to simply understand the narratives. Police must understand why certain narratives resonate in a given community. This knowledge requires police to ask questions about the history of the community, understand its culture, and listen to individual stories and perceptions whenever possible.

---

[5] A master narrative is a transhistorical narrative that is deeply embedded in a particular culture. Narratives make up a coherent system of stories that share a common rhetorical desire to resolve a conflict by establishing audience expectations according to the known trajectories of literary and rhetorical form. All master narratives are narratives, but not all narratives are master narratives. See Jeffry R. Halverson et al., *Master Narratives of Islamist Extremism* (New York: Palgrave Macmillan, 2011).

[6] Shadi Hamid, "The Roots of the Islamic State's Appeal," *Atlantic,* November 14, 2015.

[7] George Packer, "Exporting Jihad," *New Yorker,* May 28, 2016.

The attitudes and reactions of people toward police are deep, not easily changed, and often unconscious.[8] Indeed, much of the power of the police comes not from the ability to use force, but from the emotions that people feel toward the police. They wield this power in their daily interactions with people, and these interactions either strengthen or weaken people's confidence in police. Police have the "power of constructing social reality" using symbols,[9] and communities tend to make decisions based on symbols that touch them emotionally, rather than on logic or a disinterested perusal of facts.[10]

Because of the emotions that are involved in police interactions, the way people react to police is not usually rational. For example, police may be doing an excellent job of reducing crime and protecting rights, but if influential community members are telling people not to trust police, then this fact may not be considered credible. This is why police effectiveness is crucial to partnerships, but it is not the only thing police should be concerned about.

Police should be taught that the public mostly sees them through an emotional, not a logical, lens. Considering the ideas of narratives and the emotional lens of the community, one way police can serve communities and build goodwill before crimes occur is through volunteer work (loosely defined). For example, the police department in Columbia Heights, Minnesota, is headed by Chief Scott Nadeau, who deploys a community-oriented strategy. A newspaper profile describes it thus:

> All officers in Nadeau's department are required to perform at least 10 hours of community policing activities every year, though he said most devote closer to 40 hours

---

[8] Cheryl Staats, *State of the Science: Implicit Bias Review 2014* (Columbus, OH: Kirwan Institute, 2014), 16.

[9] Nick Couldry, *Media, Symbolic Power, and the Limits of Bourdieu's Field Theory* (London: London School of Economics and Political Science, 2003).

[10] As Robert Jervis explains, "The need to fit data into a wider framework of beliefs, even if doing so does not seem to do justice to individual facts, is not, or at least is not only, a psychological drive that decreases the accuracy of our perception of the world but is 'essential to the logic of inquiry.'" See Robert Jervis, "Hypotheses on Misperception," *World Politics* 20, no. 3 (1968): 457.

to the work. Officers are encouraged to choose activities that match their skills and interests. There are many choices: conducting CPR trainings, answering questions at classes for recent immigrants, serving food at a church's community dinner or holding "Coffee with a Cop" open hours, where residents are free to speak their minds with officers.

Nadeau admits that community policing "wasn't always popular with [officers]; it took months or years for some people to see the value." He notes that the department took care to introduce new initiatives slowly. "But I think even the officers we had that were more traditional saw the changes in the relationships between our police department and the community."[11] Over time, police got to know community members better, resulting in an improved view of citizens.

Because problem solving and true partnership require willingness and investment from both communities and police, confidence-building activities that can positively affect both parties' attitudes are vital. They allow police to get to know community members, understand the narratives that exist in communities, and broaden their view of members of the public so they are seen as not simply threats. These kinds of activities also lay the groundwork for community members' willingness to come to police with information to solve problems together and to rely on the police when crimes occur.

With knowledge of why narratives matter for public confidence, the emotional underpinnings of the public perception of police, and how community engagement can affect public confidence, officers will have the intellectual background to be proactive in dealings with community members. Police will see community members as a source of strength, as people who are also concerned with addressing local problems that could grow into larger ones. Police will have an inherent incentive structure for increasing the number of partnerships they form, and they will understand that their attempts to touch public emotions are as important as crime

---

[11] Kate Abbey-Lambertz and Joseph Erbentraut, "The Simple Strategies that Could Fundamentally Change How Communities View Their Police," *Huffington Post*, December 7, 2017.

statistics. These attitudes, in turn, will foster the public confidence that is required for two pillars of CVE efforts: building partnerships and joint problem solving. Moreover, police will have the knowledge to utilize skills (presented in part IV) to determine which community members are likely to be supporters of violent extremists. They will know how narratives in the community circulate and what matters to community members with respect to police-community relations. Police will be better equipped to deal with misunderstandings that come to the surface as they arise, rather than being caught off guard. Finally, as a by-product of positive engagement, members of the public will be more likely to come to police with information when they believe police understand them.

Change Perceptions of Police Response

Historically, police work has been about responding to crime. Without doubt, responsiveness to calls is vital, but it often overshadows more proactive strategies related to problem solving and partnerships. This is entirely understandable: response time is measurable and thus lends itself to improvement (faster cars, better communications systems, and so forth). Also, police availability and responsiveness leave an impression on the public's confidence in police and their role.

Frontline officers and those teaching them need to understand the points about narrative and emotions discussed above, because whenever police interact with members of the public, they are contributing to confidence building or confidence breaking. Consider two fundamental questions that people around the world ask themselves when calling the police: "If I call the police, will they come?" and "If I call the police, will they make the situation better or worse?"

The first question centers on whether police are available and willing to respond to a call. Indeed, people opposed to COP strategies have made the argument that if police are spending their time getting to know communities, their response time and efficiency will be diminished. In a COP paradigm, responding to calls may take priority over proactive strategies when dealing with immediate needs, but officers must spend time being oriented toward the community as well. In this way, COP is an operational orientation and an organizational ethos rather than a set of discrete tasks. Police should be available to respond to calls because that is when people feel they need them—if police are not there when they are needed, or it takes overly long for them to arrive, future efforts to form partnerships and confidence in general will be at risk.

The public must know how to reach the police. Methods include not only emergency and nonemergency numbers to call, but also being visible to the public. The extent to which police should be walking the beat (as opposed to patrolling in their vehicles, or, perhaps, on horseback) depends on the society in question. But simply being visible is part of being available and contributing to the public sense that police are there and will help when called upon.

For example, in 2007 there was no local Police Service of Northern Ireland (PSNI) station in New Lodge, a predominantly republican area. The PSNI also lacked a Neighbourhood Policing Team, a unit specifically responsible for community engagement. One study sums up the public's perception:

> Generally, the view appeared to be that the PSNI took an inordinately long time to respond to calls for assistance, was not remotely interested in tackling issues around local crime and anti-social behavior, engaged in mainly reactive policing, was more interested in recruiting informers ("touts") and officers were never around when they were needed. As such, the perception of the GNLCEP [Greater New Lodge Community Empowerment Partnership] was that dissident republican groups were capitalizing on community concerns about crime and neighborhood disorder in order both to [make] legitimate attacks on police officers and engage in extra-legal punishment attacks on offenders.[12]

---

[12] Graham Ellison, Nathan Pino, and Peter Shirlow, "Assessing the Determinants of Public Confidence in the Police: A Case Study of a Post-Conflict Community in Northern Ireland," *Criminology & Criminal Justice* 13, no. 5 (November 8, 2012): 552–576.

PSNI officers were perceived as unavailable and unresponsive. This perception, combined with the public's view that police engaged with them only to gather intelligence and had a historical legacy of heavy-handed tactics, contributed to an overall lack of confidence in police. When illegitimate groups engaged in vigilante justice and directly attacked police, the lack of community confidence in police allowed for dissident Republican groups—violent extremists—to fill the power vacuum with acquiescence or outright support from the community.[13] It can be inferred that a lack of awareness of community perception of the police made it more difficult to form partnerships and tackle the roots of crime and discontent.

It is important for police to have plans for responding to terrorist attacks. These might include standard operating procedures for securing a crime scene, saving victims, and preventing "double-tap attacks" (i.e., attacks in which a second bomb is timed to explode when first responders are helping victims of a first explosion). These actions, as well as follow-on actions to investigate crimes and denounce violence, are crucial for shoring up police legitimacy. When violent extremists carry out an attack, the public will see police as the legitimate alternative to violent extremists. If police have confidence in the community, they will be less likely to take a forcible response to an attack, which is one of the goals of violent extremists: to provoke officers to respond in a way that aggrieves people, thereby radicalizing individuals and fueling grievances. If the public is confident that police are on their side, then police will be able to take a more creative and thoughtful response based on partnerships created before any attacks. Police need to remember that violent extremists, who are usually less well-trained and equipped than police, want police to overreact by using force to feed into the extremists' narrative of legitimacy.

When officers have communication skills and have laid the groundwork for the community to see them as on their side, the community will perceive police use of force as a last resort, used for the protection of people and places. Police, even when they respond to violent extremist attacks with force, will have positioned themselves so their actions result in increased public confidence.

---

[13] Ibid.

Knowledge about how availability and responsiveness contribute to public confidence in policing should be given to every officer; officers need to understand that they are organizational ambassadors. Their actions in public situations will affect how individuals view police in the future.

Treat All Community Members Fairly

Although police must be proactive to increase public confidence, and they must be available to react to events when they occur, how they treat people is also important. This includes during the response to a call, as well as in follow-on procedures such as detention and contact with the larger justice system. It is crucial to underscore the importance of fair treatment not only when police respond to calls from the public but in any interaction with the public, including during crime prevention. Police can take certain technical approaches during and after responding to calls that show members of the public that they place fairness as a central part of forging a just society.

The concept of procedural justice is central to understanding how fairness in dealing with members of the community affects confidence in police. As David Bayley and Robert Perito summarize, "Fairness consists of being given an opportunity to state one's case, to react to information that authorities possess, and to be treated with dignity. In short, the legitimacy of legal authorities is enhanced if they demonstrate that they are sincere in striving to be fair and just in their dealings with individuals."[14] In a procedural justice approach, police operate according to the following principles: individuals have a voice, police make decisions neutrally, police treat people with dignity and respect, and trust exists between police and community members.[15] These principles are displayed differently depending on the culture, but actions related to fairness reflect the attitude that police show toward members of the community to whom they respond.

When police treat people fairly or unfairly, they are indicating how the government regards people as individuals and as part of society. If police

---

[14] Bayley and Perito, "The Police in War," 99.
[15] Tracey Meares, "Procedural Justice: The Secret Ingredient?" (presentation of the conference Community Justice 2014, San Francisco, April 23, 2014).

officers are partial toward someone because of ethnicity, religion, or some other identity marker and do not enforce the law against that person, but then turn around and enforce it against someone else, that sends a message of injustice. It tells the one person that he or she is privileged, and the other that he or she is less than the first. This imbalance can lead to grievances against the police and the wider government. If there is no recourse for those grievances, the affected individual might conclude that violence is the only resort.

The concept of fairness, which is intertwined with the idea of justice in the criminal justice system writ large, is put into practice differently across societies. Further, the expectations that people have about being treated fairly matter a great deal in whether fair treatment increases confidence in the police. Regardless, the public cannot have confidence in police as an organization that stands for all people in society if the perception exists that police treat certain groups better than others.

During police encounters, officers should be trained to employ a set of procedures and a "police for others" attitude that inform all actions. Although these are not by themselves sufficient to build robust public confidence in police, one large meta-study found that when police use procedural justice principles in encounters with the public, the perceived legitimacy of the police increases.[16] In the United States, a study on the willingness of Muslim Americans to cooperate with police on counterterrorism measures found that the greater the perceptions of procedural justice, the greater the perceived legitimacy, as well as the greater the willingness to cooperate. Interestingly, this held true no matter how effective the demographic group perceived police to be or the severity of the terrorist threat.[17]

Findings like this underscore the fact that one-on-one encounters with police shape individuals' perceptions about the legitimacy of the police in general. Moreover, people will form opinions about legitimacy irrespective of independent evaluations of police effectiveness and will be informed

---

[16] Lorraine Mazerolle et al., "Legitimacy in Policing," *Crime Prevention Research Review,* no. 10 (June 2013): 25.

[17] Tom R. Tyler et al., "Legitimacy and Deterrence Effects in Counterterrorism Policing: A Study of Muslim Americans," *Law & Society Review* 44, no. 2 (2010): 365–402.

by existing narratives and emotions. This does not imply that responding to calls effectively and forming partnerships before crimes occur are not important. They are, because people also make determinations about legitimacy based on these interactions. But treating people fairly during and after police response, even if the outcome is not what the person would prefer, like detention, is fundamental to increasing public perceptions of police legitimacy.

Police reformers should understand that procedural justice cannot be the only way to approach organizational change. How police are portrayed in the media and pop culture, for example, can have an effect on public perceptions of legitimacy. Police must also fully understand the competing narratives of violent extremists. Procedural justice measures are enticing because they can be distilled into standard operating procedures for officers who come in direct contact with members of the public. However, these procedures cannot be implemented in isolation from a broader community-oriented ethos, nor should they be used simply as a means to an end. True partnership with community members, and authentic treatment of members of the community with dignity and fairness, can be accomplished only with a shift in attitudes toward seeing the public as the root of police strength.

Conclusion

Police officers must realize that how they treat individuals can signal to minorities, deviants (deviancy is discussed in the next chapter), and marginalized people that they are included in society rather than signaling criminality or further marginalizing them. Because police are representative of the government, they should understand that how police treat people is taken by those people as a sign of how the wider government perceives them.

Take the principle of giving people voice. If a police officer takes the time to let a person explain his or her case and why he or she may have committed a minor infraction, this signals that the officer cares enough to listen to the person's story. Treating people fairly is not a panacea for violent extremism, but it is an important concept for a police officer to understand: if an officer gives certain individuals special treatment or discriminates against others, then grievances against the entire police force grow. People tend to want to rectify injustice and may be more likely to seek justice through use of violence or support for violent extremists.

Procedural justice is a way to increase the confidence, and therefore the legitimacy, of police. Reformers cannot use it in isolation from the broader and deeper tenets of a community-oriented ethos, nor can police use it toward unjust ends. Police fairness is a component of how the public determines confidence in police.

Building on the lessons from this chapter, the next chapters focus on two additional areas of understanding crucial for officers: the root causes of crime and violence and differentiating between behavior and identity.

CHAPTER 8

UNDERSTAND THE ROOT CAUSES OF VIOLENCE

Police recruits who are knowledgeable about the economic, emotional, social, and historic ingredients of violence, as well as the societal response to convicted criminals, will be well placed to understand what may lead a person to commit a violent act. This can also include the cases of individuals convicted for violent extremist offences. Although police may not be able to directly influence any of the root causes of violence, a better understanding of these factors will help officers develop a compassionate response and problem-solving skills. This chapter discusses the drivers of criminality, RLVE and the adoption of violent extremism to highlight the importance of incorporating this knowledge into the decision-making processes of individual police officers and entire police institutions.

Impact of Module's Inclusion

An understanding of the root causes of violence creates a broader perspective on the myriad ways in which a person may decide to pursue or be pushed into violent criminal behavior. In addition, it allows an officer to proactively think about possible ways to intervene in the individual and societal factors that might lead someone to criminality. In turn, understanding these factors can also help in the recovery and reintegration into society of offenders. Grasping this background is key to engaging with the community in an empathetic manner, because violent crime is rarely committed for no reason or as a deliberate affront to society's rule of law. Rather, people often turn to crime due to a lack of understanding of alternative options.[1]

Understanding the background and outlook of such individuals may significantly influence the way in which officers interact with them. When observing deviant behavior, an officer may opt to direct the person toward local employment assistance, social service agencies, or educational opportunities, rather than waiting for him or her to potentially engage in anti-social behaviors or even criminal activity. In doing so, the officer would help the individual address the underlying issues using a problem-solving approach which can contribute to prevention of a potential criminal behavior.

Police officers are public servants and therefore are expected to be advocates for the communities in which they work, ensuring that the voices of the community are heard and taken into consideration by operational and strategic decision makers within the police institution. Police who are educated about the factors within a community as well as personal circumstances that may contribute to citizens fully embracing violent extremism are better equipped to intervene, before the opportunity for violence presents itself. With their unique position in the community, officers can address areas of local anxiety, taking measures to provide or suggest resources (as appropriate and available) and strengthen the sense of community to reduce the likelihood of violent extremism.

Impact of Module's Omission

Historically, strong policing has been measured through quantifiable results such as the number of arrests made or tickets issued.[2] Without

---

[1] Eamonn Carrabine et al., *Criminology: A Sociological Introduction*, 2nd ed. (London: Routledge, 2009).

[2] Gerasimos A. Gianakis and G. John Davis, "Reinventing or Repackaging Public Services? The Case of Community-Oriented Policing," *Public Administration Review* 58, no. 6 (1998): 485–498.

education on the underlying causes of violence, officers are ill equipped to respond to opportunities to prevent violent crime- to include violent extremist acts- and will instead spend their time seeking to address only the immediate crimes to which they respond. Officers may be unable to distinguish between, on the one side, their preconceived understandings of what criminality looks like and, on the other side, behavior that runs contrary to established societal norms.

The lack of robust knowledge about deviant activity and how to differentiate between deviance and delinquency can hinder the ability of officers to appropriately recognize deviance. ("Deviance" describes an action that may be formally enacted (such as committing a crime) or informal, as in the violations of social norms. "Delinquency" refers more directly to a violation of legal statues.)[3] This, in turn, may cause difficulty when officers must make split-second decisions about whether criminal activity has occurred. Officers run the risk of equating the appearance of perceived deviant behavior with criminality, arresting or detaining individuals for behaving in ways perceived as a threat to the security of the community. This misuse of power and inappropriate display of authority may further the divide between the police and the community, damaging the institutional reputation of the police force and heightening a sense of injustice within the community.

A dearth of attention to the root causes of violence might impact an officer's ability to determine which of two areas to respond to in times of distress: a community in which violent behavior has often occurred in the past or one without a widespread history of violent criminal activity. Lacking a robust understanding of the systemic issues that may contribute to violence, the officer might be under the impression that he or she is better off intervening in the area without a history of violent crime, and that violence is part and parcel of life in the other community. Heightened police attention in areas without widespread violence may reinforce the sense of safety within a particular jurisdiction, with an abundance of officers reducing the opportunity or likelihood for new crime to be committed. However, when police ignore circumstances of violence in

---

[3] See J. Scott and G. Marshall, *A Dictionary of Sociology,* 3rd ed. (New York: Oxford University Press, 2005).

communities where violence is common, marginalized communities may feel slighted, as though the police are unable or unwilling to represent them and preserve or rebuild their sense of safety. This lack of attention from the police force may create an opening that vigilante groups can fill.

An officer who lacks a robust understanding of the negative impact of detaining someone for a petty or first-time offense may contend that arresting the individual is the most effective way of preventing crime. This way of thinking is consistent with deterrence theory,[4] which contends that by arresting someone for a minor or first offense, one deters them from committing more serious crimes, providing the individual the opportunity to realize the error of his or her ways.[5] Unfortunately, saddled by that initial criminal conviction, the individual may be unable to pursue alternative, legitimate avenues within society. The label may impact the ability to seek employment, procure social services, and civically engage in the community. By understanding the effect of the criminal label on an individual, police officers are more inclined to pursue alternative courses of action so as to ensure that individuals are not stigmatized as a potentially violent felon.

Without an understanding of and appreciation for criminological theories, officers run the risk of grouping all criminals in the same category and ignoring the social nuances of the communities in which they operate. By including this module in the training program for police recruits, academy instructors can underscore the importance of understanding one's community and highlight ways in which it is possible for officers to assist in mitigating the likelihood of violent extremism.

---

[4] Deterrence is the use of punishment to stop potential criminals from committing crimes. Cesare Beccaria, an eighteenth-century criminologist, theorized that criminals choose to break the law only after considering the risks and rewards of their actions. The theory is that when the punishment for committing a certain crime outweighs the reward, the criminal will not commit the crime. When the punishment is viewed as less severe than the possible reward, offenders will be more likely to take a risk and commit a crime. See Cesare Beccaria, *On Crimes and Punishment* (1764).

[5] Carrabine et al., *Criminology*, 296.

Themes of Instruction

Distinguish between Deviance and Delinquency

This module aims to strengthen the distinction between deviant and delinquent behavior, reducing the negative stereotype associated with deviance to ensure that all behavior and identities are viewed without stigma and allowing officers to respond in an appropriate fashion to legitimate crime. Deviance is not an absolute ruling of right and wrong, but rather a value judgement that may help someone determine whether the actions of another are appropriate in a certain setting. Deviance is a frame of reference through which people make value judgements on the actions of others. All members of society adopt this lens, often unconsciously, when morally evaluating the behavior of those with whom they come into contact.[6] Nearly everyone has been involved in an activity viewed as deviant by another person, with varying degrees of seriousness and criminality.[7]

This lens is particularly useful to a police officer when determining the criminality of observed behaviors. Behavior that is interpreted and viewed as deviant is not necessarily criminal; making this distinction and understanding the subject of deviance will aid an officer in reacting and responding appropriately to the diverse needs of the community.

For example, in many parts of the world, tattoos and body modifications are widely perceived to be accoutrements of the criminal groups. This bias often contributes to officers targeting a person with tattoos just because the officers have been socialized in some way to make a link between tattoos and criminality. And the influence of this bias in the police's decision-making process can lead to excessive targeting, searches, and other activities that do more harm than good to the police's reputation within the community for impartiality and fairness.

Other cultural biases can similarly predisposition officers to wrongly associate a person or a group with criminal behavior. In one city, women who worked night shifts in a bar were viewed with suspicion by the local

---

[6] Erich Goode, *Deviant Behavior: An Interactionist Approach* (Englewood Cliffs, NJ: Prentice-Hall, 1978).

[7] Ibid.

police due to the belief that they were also involved in prostitution. A police officer with a personal connection to one local bartender tackled this issue and was able to put to rest the perceived criminality of this legitimate career, ensuring that women could work in the local bar unencumbered by fear of unnecessary police attention. With a more robust understanding of the variety of ways deviance may present itself, an officer will be better equipped to recognize his or her own bias against individuals who present themselves in ways that may run contrary to the wider socially accepted way of doing things.

Understand Ideology

Ideology is the framework through which one views the world to make sense of one's surroundings. It "refers to the production and representation of ideas, values, and beliefs and the way they are expressed and lived out by both individuals and groups."[8] As part of understanding ideology, an officer must recognize the role of networks in reinforcing beliefs; someone may have an extremist ideology, but it is not until they are among like-minded individuals that the shift to participating in violent activity may occur.[9]

Be Careful of Criminal Labeling

Although everyone uses labels, some labels are more detrimental than others. By taking someone guilty of a petty crime off the street and depriving that person of the opportunity to commit more crimes, an officer might be unwittingly giving that individual a lifetime sentence.[10] Through that initial conviction, the individual might receive a criminal record and be separated from family and sources of employment. Upon

---

[8] P. McLaren, "Critical Pedagogy: A Look at the Major Concepts," in *The Critical Pedagogy Reader*, 2nd ed., edited by Antonia Darder et al. (New York: Routledge, 2008), 69–96.

[9] R. Kim Cragin, "Resisting Violent Extremism: A Conceptual Model for Non-Radicalization," *Terrorism and Political Violence* 26, no. 2 (December 7, 2013): 337–353.

[10] John E. Conklin, *Criminology*, 9th ed. (Boston: Allyn and Bacon, 1998).

release, the person will be expected to pursue a legitimate lifestyle, but wearing the label of "convict" or "felon" reduces options for employment and hinders the ability to secure social services and stable housing. This may potentially further isolate the person from members of the established community. The individual may feel that he or she has no recourse but to resume participating in criminal activity and may begin associating with delinquents, increasing the likelihood of a subsequent arrest and further incarceration, feeding into the recidivistic cycle of the criminal justice system.

Criminal labeling has been applied to entire communities, in part to justify police response rates to certain neighborhoods. Some officers might be less inclined to respond to an area historically labeled as criminal. They may fear a greater workload and resulting paperwork, and may believe that intervention will have little to no impact on the overall safety of the area; they may also want to avoid unnecessary risk to themselves.[11] By utilizing labels in this way, officers lessen hopes for an increased police presence in the stigmatized community—an increase that might in fact reduce levels of criminality and help the community shake off its stigma. The officers also perpetuate or even widen the divide between police and the community. A void is created for vigilante groups to fill. By understanding the impact of labeling on both the individual and the community, an officer will be more inclined to help both individuals and entire communities avoid or escape stigmatization and thereby be better able to avoid radicalization.[12]

Identify Individual Exclusion

Due to real or perceived social or moral differences, an individual may not feel part of the larger society in which he or she exists.[13] A person may feel mentally or socially at odds with peers and believe that the community

---

[11] Douglas A. Smith, "The Neighborhood Context of Police Behavior," *Crime and Justice* 8 (1986): 313–341.

[12] Stephanie A. Wiley and Finn-Aage Esbensen, "The Effect of Police Contact," *Crime & Delinquency* 62, no. 3 (July 12, 2013): 283–307.

[13] The idea of anomie refers to a lack of normal ethical or social standards. See Émile Durkheim, *The Division of Labor in Society* (1893).

is unable to provide direction to aid in individual growth. This sense of isolation occurs at the group level as well as at the individual level.

At the community level, shared values and understanding may not exist or may not have been created between different factions occupying a shared space. When there is no common consensus in regard to what success looks like, either within the community or across communities, striving to better oneself may be viewed as futile. At the individual level, one may feel as though he or she has no role in the larger community and reject opportunities to establish social bonds. When social integration decreases, extreme deviance and crime rates increase.[14] Acknowledging and being able to identify communities and individuals that display signs of social exclusion helps officers to foster a sense of community, thereby helping people work together to create a shared identity.

Address Social Marginalization

Sources of social marginalization may include religion, race, intellect, and economic viability, among others. Marginalized individuals are shunted to the sidelines of society, often by those in the majority, denied access to mainstream social life and deprived of the possibility of financial advancement and material gains.[15] They are denied a seat at the proverbial table, ensuring that their voices are not heard. The lack of communication further isolates them from conventional society and contributes to a legacy of mistrust and disenfranchisement.

When communities are marginalized, they may not have access to, or be able to afford, adequate health care and education. Students may not feel as though they have options and may choose to drop out of school due to financial concerns or because formal education is not prioritized or seen as feasible. Upon trying to enter the workforce, they may be deemed unfit for conventional employment and forced to pursue illegitimate or atypical work. Without appropriate knowledge, individuals may have less control over when

---

[14] Wiley and Esbensen, "The Effect of Police Contact."

[15] Iris Young, "Oppression, Privilege, and Resistance: Theoretical Perspectives on Racism, Sexism, and Heterosexism," in *Oppression, Privilege, and Resistance: Theoretical Perspectives on Racism, Sexism, and Heterosexism*, ed. Lisa M. Heldke and Peg O'Connor (New York: McGraw-Hill, 2004), 41–42.

they have children, bringing new life into a cycle of diminished economic opportunity. Even those who do not pursue a life of violent activity face stigmas associated with their marginalized status within society.

The concept of social marginalization is key for officers to be aware of as they approach and interact with communities that are not seen as part of the mainstream. This understanding will afford officers greater empathy in their interactions with repeat offenders, who may not see themselves as having any alternatives to a life of crime. An understanding of the cyclical nature of marginalization may encourage officers to advocate for and help to institutionalize work training and skills-building classes within the criminal justice system. These measures may set those who have been incarcerated up for success upon their release, enabling them to pursue legitimate forms of employment.

Recognize the Role of Economic Opportunity

A historical record of unequal access to economic and employment opportunity by some social groups may lead members of those groups to harbor a negative view of the government and a feeling of disenfranchisement. As one researcher has explained: "Expectations are the goods and conditions of life to which people think they are rightfully entitled, and capabilities are the goods and conditions of life they believe they can attain and maintain in the current social system. The discrepancy between the two is called relative deprivation."[16] An individual who experiences frustration on behalf of the group to which he or she belongs is more likely to commit violent acts than someone who experiences frustration aimed at him or her as an individual.[17]

Appreciating that economic opportunity may not be equal across or within communities may help officers understand the lack of legitimate employment that may be available to certain individuals or groups of citizens. This understanding may encourage officers to become advocates for economic growth and for greater economic opportunities for marginalized groups.

---

[16] Conklin, *Criminology*.

[17] Paul K. Davis and Kim Cragin, *Social Science for Counterterrorism* (Washington, DC: RAND, 2009).

Conclusion

As a potential factor in RLVE, ideology can play a part in isolating an individual or introducing a person to like-minded members of society. How a disenfranchised mindset could feed into violence down the line is a key radicalization factor for officers to understand. This comprehension allows officers to be more alert to potential radicalizing indicators and enables them to better determine if or when intervention is necessary. With a deep understanding of how a set of ideas was born, officers are better equipped to identify ways in which to bolster the positive impressions that community members may have of police officials by modeling their behavior in a respectful and responsive manner.

By demonstrating this knowledge, officers may be better able to identify leaders who might help individuals to resist recruitment into violent extremist organizations and help law enforcement determine appropriate avenues and settings to further amplify those messages. Although individual police officers may not be able to control the host of causes of crime and violence within their jurisdiction, a greater understanding of these elements will help them better respond to and anticipate the potential for criminality. By providing additional learning avenues for messages of peace and tolerance, an opportunity may be created to prevent violent extremist messages from taking root and ensuring that deradicalization efforts will not be needed.[18]

---

[18] Ibid.

CHAPTER 9
SUPPORT DIVERSE IDENTITIES

Police officers who understand how a person defines and presents himself or herself are better equipped to recognize how their own individuality influences interactions with the public and how identity constructs influence the response of the community to them as officers. This chapter highlights the importance of police officers recognizing their own identities in order to appreciate the diverse needs and networks that exist within the public space.

As discussed in chapter 5, existing training curricula often devote only a limited amount of training hours to addressing ways to police the community in a fair and equal manner. Training may take different shapes: some academies highlight the diversity of the cultural composition of their community, others emphasize fair and equal treatment of the population regardless of their race or religion. Sometimes referred to as "prejudice-reduction training" or "antibias training," training of this nature results in an increased understanding of different social demographics and related social concerns—but rarely results in altering long-standing attitudes and behaviors.[1]

Training that overlooks or emphasizes inappropriate facets of diversity contributes to identity-based profiling, potential abuse of minorities, and an unequal representation of minorities in the criminal justice system. This, in turn, impacts the perception of the police force by the community, especially those community members from a minority

---

[1] Katherine Spencer, Amanda Charbonneau, and Jack Glaser, "Implicit Bias and Policing," *Social and Personality Psychology Compass* 10, no. 1 (2016): 58.

background who view police more negatively than those from nonminority backgrounds. [2] Current police training provides limited lessons on the importance of treating everyone equally as a technique to ensure officers are not accused of profiling or discriminatory practices.

Yet, the concept of equal treatment across the board does not take into account or appreciate the unique identities of both the police force and the community. Officer must recognize the identity of both themselves and the people with whom they interact and understand how that identity, in the moment and historically, may influence perceptions of and responses to the police officer as an authority figure.

Some observers contend that rather than focusing on what separates us, we should recognize what unites us as members of a community; in other words, it is more useful to pay attention to shared identities than to individual differences.[3] However, focusing on unifying factors can contribute to overlooking an individual's unique characteristics and specific needs and challenges. If officers are taught to treat everyone the same, they are likely to discount the importance of how each individual sees himself or herself, which is not just as a representative of one or more groups but as a unique person.

If police academies educate recruits about recognizing and acknowledging their own biases and appreciating the identities of others, officers will be more mindful of what drives their actions, understanding how identities are formed as well as how their own perceptions of and reactions to different identities develop over time. Equipped with these skills, officers will better understand the multiple ways in which individuals identify and represent themselves, an understanding that will aid them in

---

[2] Tom R. Tyler and Jeffrey Fagan, "Legitimacy and Cooperation: Why Do People Help the Police Fight Crime in Their Communities?" *Ohio State Journal of Criminal La*w 6 (2006): 231–275; Marg Liddell et al., "Over-Represented and Misunderstood: Pacific Young People and Juvenile Justice in NSW," *Australian & New Zealand Journal of Criminology* 50, no. 4 (September 13, 2016): 529–547; and Cynthia J. Najdowski et al., "Stereotype Threat and Racial Differences in Citizens' Experiences of Police Encounters," *Law and Human Behavior* 39, no. 5 (June 1, 2015): 463–477.

[3] Fathali M. Moghaddam, "The Omnicultural Imperative," *Culture & Psychology* 18, no. 3 (2012): 304–330.

responding in a fair and just way to calls for service from all demographic groups. In responding in a way that is free from negative discrimination, officers will be viewed as fair and just service providers, able to tailor their responses to the diverse needs of their community, and therefore worthy of partnering efforts.

This module helps ensure that police officers have the necessary knowledge base to meet the needs and expectations of community members. Better awareness of and respect for the diverse identities of all those within a community will lead to improved relations between the police and the individuals with whom they come into contact, including those who have been historically hard to reach or marginalized. Rather than perceiving the diversity of the community as a threat, police officers can shift their thinking to view diversity as a source of strength. By recognizing and appreciating the multitude of identities that exists within a community, officers will be better able to identify vital indicators at the moment of response to an event or in a problem-solving scenario.

Impact of Module's Inclusion

Partnerships

Social psychologists have shown that by gaining knowledge, skills, and motivation, individuals can be made aware of their unconscious biases, enabling and motivating them to activate controlled responses to counteract biases. [4] This training teaches police officers to question themselves to determine and dismantle inaccurate and discriminatory behavior and beliefs in order to rebuild their worldviews based on new perspectives grounded on mutual understanding and equality. The goal here is not to eliminate biases but to work effectively with them, understanding how biases may color one's interpretations of and responses to specific occurrences. By focusing on bias recognition rather than bias elimination, the onus is placed on the individual to continue to counter the historical legacy of biased thinking and behavior.

It is an accepted tenet of community policing that when police forces reflect the communities they serve, they have an easier time building trust and conveying a sense of equity to the public,[5] and are better able to defuse rather than escalate tense situations.[6] In recent years, attempts have been made to gradually transform the spirit of a discriminatory police force by encouraging the recruitment of officers from more diverse backgrounds so that the force reflects the makeup of the community as a whole. In doing so, the law enforcement community acknowledges the variety of needs and expectations of different demographics and seeks to have more identities represented and better understood going forward. Although this is a strong first step, it is based on the assumption that, for

---

[4] Irene V. Blair et al., "Imagining Stereotypes Away: The Moderation of Implicit Stereotypes through Mental Imagery," *Journal of Personality and Social Psychology* 81, no. 5 (Nov. 2001): 828–841; Dasgupta Nilanjana and Anthony G. Greenwald, "On the Malleability of Automatic Attitudes: Combating Automatic Prejudice with Images of Admired and Disliked Individuals," *Journal of Personality and Social Psychology* 81, no. 5 (2001): 800–814; P. G. Devine and M. J. Monteith, "The Role of Discrepancy-Associated Affect in Prejudice Reduction," in *Affect, Cognition, and Stereotyping: Interactive Processes in Group Perception,* ed. David L. Hamilton and Diane M. Mackie (New York: Academic Press, 1993), 317–344; and E. Ashby Plant and Patricia G. Devine, "The Active Control of Prejudice: Unpacking the Intentions Guiding Control Efforts," *Journal of Personality and Social Psychology* 96, no. 3 (March 2009): 640–652.

[5] Lorie Fridell, and Mary Ann Wycoff, eds., *Community Policing: The Past, Present, and Future* (Baltimore, MD: Annie E. Casey Foundation; Washington, DC: Police Executive Research Forum, November 2004).

[6] Shaila Dewan, "Mostly White Forces in Mostly Black Towns: Police Struggle for Racial Diversity," *New York Times,* September 9, 2014.

example, only a Muslim-identifying officer is equipped to arrest a Muslim-identifying member of the community or a white Caucasian male is best deployed to respond to a call for service from a white Caucasian male.

Although issues of recruitment are integral to a diverse, representative police force, this approach—if employed without additional training—means that the individual identities of community members are discounted under the premise that one shared identity marker creates a shared identity. For example, this hiring model implicitly—and inaccurately—assumes that the hiring of one female officer allows the entire police service to know and understand the needs of all females within the community, irrespective of the many other characteristics that might define them.

All officers should be able to speak to and understand the diversity of needs and expectations of the community. Training recruits to understand the community and to build better relationships with people from different backgrounds, coupled with the other modules presented in this book, is a solution to this institutional challenge.[7]

Unchecked biased behavior in policing jeopardizes how officers are perceived and their ability to respond appropriately in times of emergency. The use of unchecked stereotypes against certain demographic markers may lead officers to be too vigilant with certain groups of people and insufficiently vigilant with others. If this happens, a risk assessment of imminent threat will be based on feelings or preconceived notions regarding a person's background rather than on facts. In prioritizing the safety of certain communities over others, officers also may open themselves up to the risk of retaliation and attack by those seeking retribution for the lack of justice for their identity group.[8]

Responding to the community in a discriminatory manner also impacts the ways in which the community responds to requests from the police, because individuals are significantly "more likely to want to cooperate with police when they feel they will be treated in a fair, respectful

---

[7] Mark Furlong and James Wight, "Promoting 'Critical Awareness' and Critiquing 'Cultural Competence': Towards Disrupting Received Professional Knowledges," *Australian Social Work* 64, no. 1 (February 24, 2011): 38–54.

[8] Douglas A. Smith, "The Neighborhood Context of Police Behavior," *Crime and Justice* 8 (1986): 313–341.

and impartial manner."[9] A police officer's safety may be increased if he or she understands how he or she perceives others and how others perceive him or her. This comprehension reduces the fear of others, as officers are encouraged to move beyond merely existing alongside other cultures and to start questioning their own values, beliefs, and behaviors.[10]

For example, an officer equipped with an understanding of his or her own identity and personal biases can take steps to look beyond the physical appearance of community members and focus on their protection. With this understanding, officers will be better equipped to build partnerships throughout the community, encouraging the development of a wider network of trusted advisors and a more localized perspective on what is happening in different parts of the community.

Organizational Culture

Historically and globally, the role of police has been occupied by men, particularly those from the ethnic majority of their communities. As an occupation in harm's way and under direct threat, policework has come to be viewed as best suited to a hyper-masculinized identity that could ensure self-protection and promote the image of protector to the community.[11] Members of the public as well as those within the police force equate effective crime response with character traits such as aggression, violence, courage, and risk taking, characteristics often deemed masculine in nature.[12] Through internal and external messaging of what it means to be an officer, the organizational culture within many police forces encourages

---

[9] Kristina Murphy and Adrian Cherney, "Understanding Cooperation with Police in a Diverse Society," *British Journal of Criminology* 52, no. 1 (August 19, 2011): 181–201.

[10] M. E. Duffy, "Issues and Innovations in Nursing Education: A Critique of Cultural Education in Nursing," *Journal of Advanced Nursing* 36, no. 4 (November 2001): 487–495.

[11] Angela Workman-Stark, "From Exclusion to Inclusion," *Equality, Diversity and Inclusion: An International Journal* 34, no. 8 (2015): 764–775.

[12] Merry Morash and Robin N. Haarr, "Doing, Redoing, and Undoing Gender," *Feminist Criminology* 7, no. 1 (August 23, 2011): 3–23.

derogatory or inflammatory small talk and joking targeting minority groups and women.[13]

This toxic workplace culture has made it difficult for those perceived as different to break into the service and feel comfortable. With appropriate training, officers can learn to examine their own identity and the way in which they talk about others, shedding light on how the words they use may be received and experienced by others. This awareness in turn fosters a workplace culture in which the backgrounds and identities of all those present are respected and valued, rather than mocked and ridiculed. Prejudice-reduction programs are most effective when integrated into the organizational culture so that all members of the organization gradually learn the new mindset and philosophy of the organization, as well as its new values and principles.[14] Although academy training should go beyond simple prejudice-reduction programs, their value to the workplace culture remains.

Working in an environment that can often be dangerous, officers often feel physically and emotionally separated from the community members they serve.[15] This sense of professional isolation may bleed into their personal lives, hindering their ability to forge strong and lasting relationships outside of the force. By encouraging an ethos of inclusion and understanding of actors and identities within a community, the academy will better equip officers to appreciate the diversity of needs in their surroundings. This understanding in turn can assist in breaking down the divisions between the police and the general population and encourage the development of relationships outside the force, in both a personal and a professional capacity.

The Community

By introducing the importance of identity and ensuring that officers are made aware of their own biases and preconceived notions of certain

---

[13] Ibid.

[14] Hill and Augoustinos, "Stereotype Change."

[15] Douglas Paton and John M. Violanti, *Traumatic Stress in Critical Occupations: Recognition, Consequences, and Treatment* (Springfield, IL: Charles C. Thomas, 1996).

demographics, recruits will have the opportunity to analyze their own understanding of what it means to exist as someone viewed as "other." With a mutual understanding of and respect for how people identify themselves, officers will feel more comfortable working with and responding to the needs of all people they come into contact with. In discussing the importance of fair and equal representation, it is crucial that all areas of the community receive the attention and focus of police to ensure that the right of protection is respected across the community.

Individuals experience their surroundings in unique ways. Recognizing personal perspectives and experiences is of the utmost importance for police officers. With different perspectives come different networks of understanding and resources of support. A mother who fears that her child is in the process of becoming radicalized may reach out to her network of mothers to share experiences, elicit advice, and voice her concerns in a space perceived as free from judgement. A father is likely to do the same with his own network of trusted peers. Each parent is experiencing the fear of the radicalization of their children in his or her own way, seeking advice and support from different networks.

In certain communities, where access to global news is not widespread, informal gatherings are often the only means for receiving local information and learning about current events. Understanding gendered identities and the related spheres of support can help police better conceptualize how information spreads throughout the environment, in turn allowing them to disseminate their own messaging and to capitalize on existing lines of support and conversation.

Cultural barriers must be understood. In certain cultures and communities, different identities are granted different access within networks. For example, in many cultures, mothers are afforded a privileged status within the home, privy to information about the goings-on, social networks, and extracurricular activity of the children. Recognizing the gender dynamics of a household can better prepare an officer to question the different actors in a situation and get a more well-rounded perspective of a family and community. If mothers have insight into the activities of young people but are discouraged from talking to, or not allowed to talk to, men outside the family, officers must recognize this reality and enlist the support of a female officer or colleague during the interview process to ensure that crucial pieces of information are not missed due to cultural barriers.

Impact of Module's Omission

Biased or discriminatory behavior from the police manifests through responses in favor of or against a given person, group, or demographic. This may create tension between people who are treated favorably by police and those who are not, undermining relations between different groups in society as well as eroding the legitimacy of the police force. Reacting to people based on their appearance will increase tensions and fuel resentment within minorities toward the police and the majority population.

Grievances That Push People toward Violent Extremism

Discriminatory or biased treatment by police may expedite the RLVE process and lead individuals to join VEOs. When officers make decisions about, and act toward, certain people based on their identity rather than on their behavior, targeted groups or individuals may feel discriminated against and alienated. For instance, they may be more likely to believe that society and/or the state does not treat them in the same way as other individuals or groups because of their ethnicity, language, ideological or religious beliefs.[16] This sense of injustice and real or perceived wrongdoing may encourage a person to seek out like-minded individuals who also feel persecuted against. The sense of social and/or political marginalization, coupled with a supportive group of individuals and an understanding that there are few or no opportunities to move beyond the current set of obstacles, may prepare the ground for the intervention of violent extremist recruiters and their narratives. This in turn may push an individual to radicalize and potentially embrace violence to ensure change.

---

[16] UN General Assembly, "Report of the Special Rapporteur on the Promotion and Protection of Human Rights and Fundamental Freedoms While Countering Terrorism, Martin Scheinin," Office of the United Nations High Commissioner for Human Rights, December 22, 2010.

Profiling and Intelligence Gathering

In an effort to engage with certain communities, some police services have encouraged officers to surreptitiously monitor the activities and goings-on of select demographics and their families, believing them to be more likely than others to engage in violent extremist activity. In doing so, officers have been accused of profiling community members, feeding into a narrative of police monitoring the activities of certain groups so as to catch them in the act of plotting or planning violent activity.

For example, many Muslim and Arab communities support the police as an institution, but believe counterterrorism laws are unfair because they are disproportionately used against Muslims and Arabs compared with other communities.[17] When communities begin to believe that officers are more concerned about catching people in the act of criminality than protecting them from it, some may come to see the police as a source not of security, but of personal and communal insecurity. According to one study of the policing of Muslim communities: "Muslim groups (in areas where they are the minority) are simultaneously over-policed as suspects and under-policed as victims, which has reduced their confidence in and willingness to collaborate with the police."[18] By including the module proposed here, officers will be better equipped to ensure that their relationship with the community is mutually beneficial and not perceived as a means for uncovering incriminating evidence.

One additional benefit of this module may be increased access to local intelligence, as officers gain the trust and confidence of their community and individuals trust that police will take appropriate action with the information given. However, it is imperative that intelligence collection be cast as a by-product of COP rather than the driving force behind it; this COP narrative will help establish and build local support of the community policing programming.

---

[17] Ibid.

[18] Hakeem et al., *Policing Muslim Communities.*

Themes of Instruction

Be Self-Aware

To better understand how an officer will be perceived by those in the community in both a professional and a personal sense, officers must self-reflect to determine both how they conceive of themselves and how others might view them as individuals and as individuals in uniform. Officers must determine how they became the person they are; what privileges or disadvantages they were afforded; their level of education, their physical ability, and their sexuality; and their conceptualization of their faith and race, among many other factors. An identity comprises a combination of these factors and may differ on a situational basis depending on the people with whom one is interacting. A person may present an identity at work that is tailored for the professional setting, and present a different identity in a social sphere.[19]

Identity is not made up of a simple label that encompasses everything that makes of an individual. Rather, identity is made up of a multitude of factors that come to the fore at different times; not just gender, but also race, religion, socioeconomic background, sexuality, and a variety of other identifying labels. Whether or not one facet of an identity is in keeping with the identity of the majority of the population may impact how visible that component is in daily interactions. A person may determine that, in an effort to fit in with the majority of the population, it is in his or her best interest to conceal or downplay certain aspects of identity. The opposite may also be true: a person may be eager to stand out from the crowd and thus amplify certain idiosyncratic elements of his or her identity.

Personal identity markers overlap with one another, crossing in and out at various times as a result of different internal and external stimuli, and they influence a person's approach and response to the world, including authority figures.[20] How we conceive of who we are is a matter of organizing and interpreting these various identities. The idea that various identities exist in each individual reminds officers to recognize and appreciate the

---

[19] Morash and Haarr, "Doing, Redoing, and Undoing Gender."

[20] Leslie Paik, "Critical Perspectives on Intersectionality and Criminology: Introduction," *Theoretical Criminology* 21, no. 1 (2017): 4–10.

many facets of their own identity as well as those with whom they may meet to ensure that they are respectful and respond to the needs of the community in a way that is equitable and just.

Recognize Bias

Implicit bias refers to the stereotypes or attitudes that have an influence on one's understanding and actions and impact the decisions one takes.[21] "These biases, which include both favorable and unfavorable assessments, are activated involuntarily and without an individual's awareness or intentional control."[22] Implicit bias is about categorizing individuals and associating them with a stereotype automatically, classifying individuals according to group membership such as gender, weight, ethnicity, sexuality, or faith.[23]

Explicit bias occurs when a person associates a group with a negative stereotype and those individuals who hold the bias are aware of and recognize their prejudices and attitudes toward certain groups.[24] Police officers who are not aware of their biases are problematic because bias influences choices and actions, negatively impacting the citizens that they come into contact with. Learning about implicit bias is perhaps more important for police officers than for members of any other profession because police are authorized to use force up to and including lethal force. Recruits must understand that their vested power combined with prejudices can have disastrous outcomes. In addition, officers must learn to recognize when they are reacting to a perceived threat based on identity

---

[21] The critical insight that race, class, gender, sexuality, ethnicity, nation, ability, and age operate not as unitary, mutually exclusive entities but as reciprocally constructing phenomena that in turn shape complex social inequalities. See P. H. Collins, "Intersectionality's Definitional Dilemmas," *Annual Review of Sociology* 41 (2015): 1–20.

[22] Staats, "State of the Science," 16.

[23] Lorie A. Fridell, *Producing Bias-Free Policing: a Science-Based Approach* (New York: Springer, 2017).

[24] Lorie Fridell, "This Is Not Your Grandparents' Prejudice: The Implications of the Modern Science of Bias for Police Training," *Translational Criminology* (Fall 2013): 10–11.

or their personal understanding of identity as opposed to responding to actual criminal behavior.

Recognizing one's own biases is an important step for officers. To more fully understand how certain biases and prejudicial ways of thinking have developed over time, officers must examine the content and the sources of messages they have received about other identities throughout their lives. By identifying their own biases, officers will gain a better understanding of who they are likely to engage with positively and who they might treat less respectfully if bias is not checked.

One method of bias inventory is the "cycle of socialization," in which an individual walks through how their own identity formation impacts feelings about and understandings of what it means to be and see others as different.[25] The cycle begins at birth, where we are introduced to our surroundings. During this nascent stage, socialization begins with those who are raising us, influencing both how we think of ourselves and how we think of and relate to others. We enter into new and different social environments as we enter school and become more active participants in our surroundings. We receive an onslaught of messages about others with whom we come into contact and the roles that are appropriate for both us and them to play. We become familiar with societal stereotypes that shape how we think and what we believe about ourselves and others. If we are part of the majority that potentially benefits from these ways of thinking, we may not notice the external injustices and how they are experienced by others. Alternatively, if we are negatively and directly impacted, we may feel attacked and under constant threat. We as individuals are presented with a choice: we may choose to do nothing and not confront the impact of our behaviors on those around us, allowing the cycle to begin again with another generation. Or we may question preexisting assumptions about how we perceive others, attempting to learn more about different backgrounds and those whose identity differs from our own in order to challenge the basis of our biases. It is only through this latter, critical approach to understanding our environment that we may attempt to

---

[25] B. Harro, "Cycle of Socialization," in *Readings for Diversity and Social Justice,* ed. Maurianne Adams, (London: Routledge, 2018), 15–21.

disrupt the cycle, which is moored to the feelings of fear, ignorance, confusion, and insecurity both of oneself and others.[26]

Through understanding and recognizing the impact of how individuals are socialized to relate to others, officers will be better able to understand how they perceive identity markers, how these markers have been reinforced over time, and the part each person can play in disrupting this cycle. This deeper understanding of how officers conceive of others will assist them in recognizing and breaking out of biased behavior. The fact that the cycle of socialization begins at birth and takes into account the impact of various actors and their views on the individual as they develop sets it apart from other attempts to understand how one comes to conceive both of oneself and of what it means to be different.

Respond to Emotionally Distressed People

Understanding the identity of oneself and the community is of crucial importance for a police officer. But what happens when an officer is unable to differentiate between behavior and identity?

Individuals with psychological disorders or under severe emotional duress may behave or react to external stimuli in ways that may be difficult for officers to predict or navigate. This population also has an increased likelihood of coming into contact with the police, and thus special attention should be paid to understanding this demographic. [27] Being able to identify and adequately respond to the needs of mentally and emotionally distressed persons can benefit police officers not only in their approach to the community but also in the way in which they respond to crisis situations.

While subsequent chapters highlight different practical skills that assist officers in responding to individuals under psychological and emotional duress, this module centers on knowledge-based training to ensure that officers are equipped to address concerns of emotionally distressed people. Factors that may emotionally distress people include psychological

---

[26] Ibid.

[27] Yasmeen I. Krameddine et al., "A Novel Training Program for Police Officers That Improves Interactions with Mentally Ill Individuals and Is Cost-Effective," *Journal of the American Academy of Psychiatry and the Law* 41, no. 3 (2013): 344–355.

disorders, substance abuse, medical conditions, situational stress, or a combination of these factors. Only through observing an individual's behavior and engaging with that person can an officer begin to understand the impetus for and the underlying cause of a crisis at hand.[28]

Officers are not and should not be expected to be mental health clinicians. It is not their responsibility to diagnose a psychological disorder or condition; their task is to identify an individual in distress and support that person in finding resources rather than mistaking them for a threat. Mistakes of that sort are costly for police legitimacy and partnerships and can help elevate extremist narratives. To respond appropriately to a situation involving a psychologically distressed person, an officer must put to use an understanding of identity markers, recognizing that the identity marker of psychological disorders is but one way in which the individual may or may not identify themselves, depending on whether or not they have been diagnosed and sought and agreed to treatment. Recognizing manifestations of emotional distress by considering physical cues, verbal indicators, and environmental triggers should be a focus of training, which should be provided by mental health practitioners from within the community and be tailored to the local context, centered around the prevalence of local mental health concerns, indicators and symptoms, and appropriate responses, as well as potential issues that may arise in custody settings.[29]

Map Social Services and Communal Identities

The final component of the module on supporting diverse identities focuses on recognizing appropriate alternate resources to supplement and complement the authority of the police force. This program of instruction has been intentionally placed at the end of the chapter to ensure that the lessons from previous components of this module inform the approach and understanding of the content included here.

---

[28] Integrating Communications, Assessment, and Tactics, *A Training Guide for Defusing Critical Incidents*, Police Executive Research Forum, October 2016.

[29] Ian Cummings and Stuart Jones, "Blue Remembered Skills: Mental Health Awareness Training for Police Officers," *Journal of Adult Protection* 12, no. 3 (August 23, 2010): 14–19.

As mentioned in the introduction to this chapter, historical attempts to liaise with local community groups have sometimes been perceived as attempts at intelligence gathering or surveillance, jeopardizing both the legitimacy of the police and local perceptions of the community organizations involved. This section highlights examples of community organizations that police officers should be aware of and the corresponding identities that they serve so that officers can understand the relationships between social services and community needs. This knowledge will equip officers to tap into local resources and be aware of potential allies to provide background or localized information, in addition to supporting those in need or at risk of radicalization.

Recognizing and working with parental influence can be particularly important for police to assist in fostering the development of resilience to violent extremism in young people. But officers must also recognize that gendered identities can shape the nature and extent of influence that different parents exercise. The spheres of influence within which women move often differ drastically from those of men. As actors traditionally more directly involved in the upbringing and home life of children, mothers may have significant influence within the social hierarchies of communities and families; however, they may not be encouraged to challenge existing public social norms.[30] Amplifying the voices of mothers and providing them with information in regard to the threat of radicalization can help empower them to play a more active role in CVE efforts.[31] Fathers may act as family and community leaders and, in certain societies, play an active role in creating new narratives surrounding concepts of masculinity and protection. Although the same resources should be offered to both parents, it is crucial to recognize the identified role that they occupy within the family and their community, and to tailor material accordingly.

Working with different community resources will further develop an officer's knowledge about the multitude of identities that exist within the local

---

[30] "Charting a New Course: Thought for Action Kit," Women Preventing Violent Extremism, United States Institute of Peace, 2015.

[31] "The Role of Families in Preventing and Countering Violent Extremism: Strategic Recommendations and Programming Options," Initiative to Address the Life Cycle of Radicalization to Violence, Global Counterterrorism Forum (GCTF), 2016.

jurisdiction and the range of ways in which to respond to cultural sensitivities. This outreach can better inform an understanding of religious and cultural nuances, ensuring that officers are aware of the diversity that exists within their precinct and better equipping them to respond and react to conflict within or between communities. For example, an officer who regularly engages with an abused women's shelter is likely to be better versed in how abuse can span socioeconomic divides and to understand that it is not only an issue for lower-income households. To take another example: an officer who works as a police liaison with social workers who focus on deradicalization will soon discover that it is not only inadequately educated young men who are seeking this professional assistance; the social workers help people from a multitude of educational backgrounds. Acting in this liaison capacity can shatter an officer's preconceived beliefs about at-risk populations.

Training should cover subjects such as how to map social services to community needs. For example, police officers being trained in Hong Kong were given an opportunity to mirror various social service providers to get a better understanding of their work, the challenges they face, and the approaches they adopt in responding to the needs of a variety of clients.[32] The results of this training were overwhelmingly positive: 98 percent of participants believed that the training would strengthen their collaboration with working with the population, and 96 percent believed that it would strengthen their understanding of the psychological needs of the community.[33] Identifying organizations within the community whose mandate it is to provide social or spiritual support will aid an officer in recognizing the limits of authority and the knowledge and impact of community partnerships.

Once appropriate social service agencies have been identified, outreach should be done on a semiregular basis to ensure that officers' presence within the community is not solely associated with times of crisis or duress. Officers can use the time devoted to outreach to learn more about the individuals in the community, increasing the officers' understanding of the population as well as the different channels of information that may exist

---

[32] Roxco P. K. Chun et al., "Police Work with Youth-At-Risk: What Can Social Work Contribute?" *Hong Kong Journal of Social Work* 44, no. 1 (2010): 31–48.
[33] Ibid.

within the area. This is also a useful way for community members to gain a greater understanding of police work and current priorities.

Conclusion

It is important for police officers to understand the personal identity of both themselves and the individuals whom they serve. By recognizing how unique markers influence one's understanding of and approach to others, at the individual and the community levels, officers can better respond to situations in an equitable manner.

Training programs and lessons focused on allowing officers the opportunity to understand both themselves and the community need to be integrated into the training of recruits and on-the job training so as to guarantee ongoing and repeated exposure to these lessons and values, emphasizing the principles of equality and social justice.[34] This reinforcement will aid officers as they reach out to their community and respond professionally to the needs of those from a wide spectrum of identities, thereby bolstering public confidence in the police.

---

[34] Miriam and Augoustinos, "Stereotype Change."

PART IV

MODULES FOR COP: DEVELOPING INTERPERSONAL SKILLS

CHAPTER 10
THE PERSONAL TOUCH

In addition to knowledge-based tools, police institutions that wish to adopt a COP ethos must pay attention to existing operational procedures that can push individuals to support or join violent extremist groups. A key asset of COP is a culture of prevention, which requires a departmental shift from a culture that prioritizes response to criminal and violent activities to one that fosters partnerships and problem-solving capacity. Training in practical skills such as communication, problem solving, and critical thinking can build officers' capacity to develop a more community-centric approach that will enhance CVE efforts. Using these skills and tools, officers can reduce community grievances based on police violence. These skills also enhance officers' ability to identify threats and address the security needs of their communities.

As explained in the next three chapters, interpersonal skills such as communication and critical thinking, negotiation, and mediation are vital for implementing COP successfully. Effective policing relies heavily on the capacity of individual officers to exercise discretion in order to remain on the nonlethal side of the continuum of force, and these skills are fundamental additions to an officer's interpersonal skillset. Teaching these skills will increase the capacity of a police officer to build and use partnerships to proactively address public safety concerns. Problem-solving techniques and analytical skills increase an officer's capacity to develop strategies to identify, prevent, and mitigate the drivers of violent extremism. These interpersonal skills encourage a proactive and collaborative relationship to address concerns identified by the community.

Contemporary policing is not merely about fighting crime. Indeed, most police activities involve providing a range of services and solving problems. Officers are often dispatched to respond to situations that do not necessitate an arrest, but rather require a professional officer who is equipped with a range of skills and techniques to peacefully settle the issue at hand. To instill a COP ethos, officers must be trained beyond traditional technical skills that are provided in the current police academy training and learn to employ interpersonal skills to solve problems, foster partnerships, and effect organizational transformation.

Solve Problems

Officers interact and communicate with all members of the community in their efforts to prevent and respond to crime and violence. Police officers must study and analyze the characteristics of problems in the area and apply all available resources to resolve them. Officers must be equipped with the skills of critical thinking, including problem conceptualization and analysis. This skillset helps them dig deep into problems to determine the underlying conditions that helped create them. An understanding of the background helps officers better connect a problem with context-specific solutions, such as linking an addict to appropriate treatment. Only skilled officers who can define a problem and create an open communication environment can explore different ways to handle difficult situations.

The skills presented in this part of the book are intended to empower officers to identify and prioritize problems and make decisions on how to best solve them as first responders and the most visible government service. Engaged community members are a valuable asset for police officers. Communities may have multiple and sometimes disputing interests that require frontline officers to act not only as enforcers of law and order but also as mediators, negotiators, and problem solvers. In the context of problem solving, police academies that train officers to interact with the community to solve the community's problems will enhance the police's CVE capacity significantly. When interacting with the community, officers must carefully asses the cost of gathering intelligence on community members. Police engagement activities are meant to build trusting relationships with community members. If police exploit this relationship, they delegitimize their authority and intentions, damaging the community's trust.

Foster Partnerships

Police alone cannot prevent crimes and make a community safe. Many solutions to and interventions in a community's problems and concerns, including preventing and countering radicalization, come from partners other than security providers. For example, a partnership between the police and health and human services departments can strengthen social cohesion within the community and provide assistance to individuals at risk of radicalization, diverting them from the path to violence.

Community partnership is the long-term goal of adopting a COP ethos. It involves sharing power and responsibilities to keep communities safe, secure, and resistant to all types of violent extremism.[1] Police officers are well positioned to build effective local networks. Officers can be a source of expertise and advice on many issues, including RLVE. Risk factors potentially contributing to RLVE include issues with identity, a desire for belonging, past trauma, personal connections to violent extremists narratives, and psychological disorders.[2] Police can more effectively address these issues in cooperation with partners such as community leaders, social service providers, and other non-law-enforcement stakeholders.[3]

Communication is the first step in building partnership. If officers do

---

[1] International Association of Chiefs of Police, *Using Community Policing to Counter Violent Extremism: 5 Key Principles for Law Enforcement*, Office of Community Oriented Policing Services, U.S. Department of Justice, 2014.

[2] National Institute of Justice, *Radicalization and Violent Extremism: Lessons Learned from Canada, the U.K. and the U.S.*, U.S. Department of Justice, Office of Justice Programs, July 2015.

[3] S. M. Weine, B. H. Ellis, R. Haddad, A. B. Miller, R. Lowenhaupt, & C. Polutnik, *Lessons Learned from Mental Health and Education: Identifying Best Practices for Addressing Violent Extremism*, Final Report to the Office of University Programs, Science and Technology Directorate, U.S. Department of Homeland Security (College Park, MD: START, 2015).

not reach out to form partnerships with community members, especially those who are distrustful of the police, those partnerships will not be made. Officers cannot simply invite community members to meetings and expect that they will show up. Typically, community members are more comfortable engaging with the police in their own neighborhoods and familiar gathering places—which is why police must go out to meet and talk with people from different backgrounds. Partnership requires that officers demonstrate not only strong tactical capabilities but also interpersonal skills that illustrate a respectful demeanor and encourage others to approach them. For example, a patrol officer needs to talk to local business owners to help identify their problem areas and concerns and participate in regular community meetings. Officers may need to explain and discuss controversial police tactics so that community members understand the necessity of or decision process behind such tactics for the community and police officer safety.

Clear and approachable language skills, coupled with other interpersonal skills, can help police to engage and build non-law enforcement partners or partners outside the security community. For example, partnerships with youth centers and education establishments can help law enforcement to engage with marginalized communities and detect and prevent radicalization. Because the youth demographic is at particular risk of falling prey to violent extremist narratives, having connections with youth in these communities will aid local law enforcement officers in disrupting the RLVE process.

Solving problems and addressing community concerns is one path to building trust and long-term meaningful relationships between police and community. Communication skills play a vital role; when officers use their skills to treat people with respect and dignity, they build trust for an effective community partnership. However, the majority of communications that officers have with the community happen during crisis situations when police are responding to emergency calls. Those situations are not always the best time for relationship building. Individuals may struggle to explain what happened, and officers are focused on finding relevant information and identifying an appropriate solution. Some community members may feel the officers are unapproachable outside of emergency contexts, or there may not be enough officers to have a reliable presence in the street. COP is about the police and community working together to address crime and quality of life issues, building a relationship, and getting to know one another when things are going well so that when things are difficult or when problems arise, people trust the police to respond effectively.

Change the Institutional Mindset

Police institutions that want to implement a COP ethos must encourage every officer to adopt a mindset of service provision and problem solving—and to see such an approach as the normal way of doing business for a frontline officer (and, indeed, for everyone else in the police institution). This calls for a shift away from the militarized, hierarchical model of traditional police institutions and toward a model in which police leadership empowers officers by delegating to them the discretionary power to respond to a situation quickly and creatively, without waiting for approval from their commanders. If officers continue to be given only limited discretionary power, they are unlikely to find effective solutions to community problems.

If officers are to be able to respond effectively to security threats, or to the problems that can spiral into such threats, they need not only greater latitude but also the skills to use that latitude wisely. Those skills include communication, self-awareness, bias recognition, and problem solving. In turn, appropriately trained police officers can effect change within the police organization by being encouraged, or even expected to, use these skills in their daily activities. Communication between an institution's leadership and its officers demonstrates respect and flattens the organizational structure, instilling a sense of trust between higher and lower ranks.

Conclusion

Building the capacity of police officers with skills-based learning helps shift the perception of police leadership to a COP ethos. Police leadership may consider community policing to consist of nothing more than a unit with a set number of tactics to be employed by individual police officers. In this structure, however, other police officers and other units are excluded from the benefits of COP. When departments build the capacity of all officers, COP is not considered to be merely a tactic assigned to certain individuals to implement but is regarded as a philosophy that covers all police activities and all officers. A department-wide COP approach reduces tension that may arise between those officers who traditionally are assigned to conduct criminal investigations and those who want to build partnerships with the community.

Teaching officers how to communicate with others, both within their own ranks and within the community, encourages them to develop creative and collaborative solutions to violence. This brings police officers into the decision-making process and helps their voices to be heard when creating new policies. It also encourages the individual to act as a driving force for improvement within the department and allows him or her to exercise the discretionary powers that are the cornerstone of professional policing.

CHAPTER 11
COMMUNICATION SKILLS

As actors on the frontlines facing the threat of violent extremism, police officers must have knowledge, skills, and attitudes that can help them in building trustful relationships with the community. Communication skills are a powerful law enforcement tool and a crucial method for building partnerships and solving problems. This chapter illustrates how communication skills—including strategic listening, verbal and nonverbal communication, and critical thinking— can be used to defuse potentially explosive situations and lower levels of violent extremism.[1]

Officers are most effective when they utilize communication skills that include verbal and nonverbal messages. These skills should be an integral part of an officer's technique for building partnerships with the community and resolving issues. The vast majority of police work involves noncriminal matters, and using the powers of arrest and incarceration are inappropriate and ineffective in those situations. Furthermore, the use of force or threatening the use of force can intimidate people into compliance and hinder the development of collaborative partnerships with the community.

Collaborative relationships between police and the community must be based on a nonthreatening and cooperative spirit. Officers should listen to community members and take seriously how individuals perceive problems and issues in the effort to solve problems. Communication skills, critical

---

[1] Shaftoe, "Dealing with Terrorist Threats."

thinking, and conflict resolution, including mediation and negotiation (covered in the next chapter), all require extensive listening.

Strategic Listening

When a person holds his or her own views rigidly and does not allow room for differing opinions, violent extremist concepts may take root.[2] When making decisions, officers should consider information from and the opinions of those who agree with them as well those who disagree, doing so with an open mind and a willingness to accept feedback or criticism.

Officers should not walk away from community members who disagree with them. Instead, they should try to enlist those community members in the collective effort to provide security for the entire community. Listening to others' voices ensures that all members of the community feel that their voices are heard in the process of creating preventive initiatives or programs.

Regardless of their assignment, be it in patrol or investigation, police normally want to do things quickly because they have so much to do on a given day. Some officers get into the habit of talking very fast and not always listening to replies. Officers should remember that when people deal with police, they are often in crisis, so officers should listen to them and make sure to speak slowly, accurately, sometimes repetitively, and always in a respectful way. Officers may believe that an individual is not cooperating with an order when in fact the person is unable to comply because of stress, illness, or disability. Officers need to take the time to listen to those with whom they interacting to better respond to their potential resistance or anger.

Strategic listening means not merely hearing what is said and gathering information, but also ensuring that the necessary and appropriate actors are engaged and participating in the conversation. Strategic listening is a way for officers to build trust and show respect to establish a professional relationship with the community. An officer who demonstrates strategic listening gives an individual full attention and focus, thereby indicating the officer's involvement and concern for what the person has to say.

Strategic listening can be demonstrated through multiple techniques that reflect the listener's active engagement in the conversation and

---

[2] Desmond Tutu, "Special Event: Extremism," *Doha Debates*, February 26, 2006.

desire for greater information. Approaches include, but are not limited to, the following:

- *Encourage*: Find areas of interest that will encourage the speaker to keep talking. Further and deeper discussion may expose root causes of a problem.

- *Elicit*: Ask open-ended questions to clarify the needs of the other person and prevent misinformation from spreading. This allows the officer the opportunity to clarify ambiguous or unfamiliar language, thereby gaining more information about the problems at hand. The use of open-ended questions (i.e., avoiding asking questions that can answered with just a "no" or a "yes") and avoiding leading questions that result in specific answers will increase the level of communication between police officer and the individual.

- *Restate*: Restate what has been communicated to show the individual that the officer is paying attention to what is being said and is trying to understand. This also creates an opportunity to determine if intended messages are in fact being received.

- *Clarify*: Ask clarifying questions to illustrate the officer's desire to accurately capture the information relayed and to test his or her interpretation of that information.

- *Empathize*: Listen to understand how the other person feels, listening not only with one's ears but also with one's eyes and heart to gain a better understanding of and feeling for the meaning of the speaker's words without judgment.

- *Summarize*: Formulate a concise overview of the key points made by the speaker in order to check that the message that is understood is consistent with the one that is intended.

- *Reframe*: Restate negative or adversarial statements in more neutral or potentially positive ways that make it possible for the officer and the speaker to find common ground.

Public Speaking

Many officers assume that because they know operational procedures well, they can speak before community audiences with little or no preparation. In truth, public speaking can be difficult. Public speaking encompasses speaking to many people at once and conversing with others.

Public speaking skills are called for at all levels of service, from police chiefs down to supervisors, investigators, and frontline officers. Police officers may be interviewed by television or radio reporters, and often they must spontaneously tell the community about their activities and operations or testify in court. Police institutions have an obligation to speak to the public and provide accurate and up-to-date information to the people they serve.

Because officers represent the entire organization, it is in the interest of police leaders to teach public speaking skills. Officers should be given opportunities to enhance their skills during constructive interactions—for example, by chairing meetings or making presentations during training sessions and receiving feedback from colleagues. Officers who are strong public speakers may play a more robust role in marketing, branding, developing, and sustaining long-term connections to people. This will enhance how police institutions are perceived by the community.

Conversational Skills

The approach taken by police officers to engage members of the community to solve problems and create partnerships can affect their reputation, legitimacy, and the degree of confidence the community has in their ability to police effectively.

As part of their conversational skills, officers need to be able to distinguish between debate and dialogue. Debates occur between two opposing sides, and the goal is to win the conversation by proving the other side wrong; the goal of dialogue is to increase the other's understanding of one's own perspective. In debate, people listen with the goal of finding mistakes and making counterarguments, whereas in dialogue people listen with the goal of understanding and finding a common language. Dialogue is a way for people to interact, hear, and understand points of view that differ from their own.

Police officers must be willing to address the root causes of a crisis, not just the symptoms on the surface, and root causes can be revealed only through dialogue.[3] When officers use open-ended questions and carefully listen to responses, they may discover new options for solving problems and will recognize that not all situations have only one right answer. Officers will get the opportunity to know, understand, and respect the perspectives of others, rather than listening in order to dismantle others' arguments and beliefs.

Police officers should be trained in the art of having difficult conversations. Conversational skills can be used as an intervention technique to de-escalate tension in crisis, to solve problems, and to address community grievances. Furthermore, officers can utilize interactive opportunities to educate citizens. Conversation can be planned or unplanned and can happen at any time, whenever and wherever officers come into contact with members of the public. Officers may miss opportunities to counter violent extremism if they do not demonstrate conversational skills.

Nonverbal Skills

Any message that a police officer wants to transmit to the citizenry has two parts: the words that are spoken and the signals that accompany the verbal communication, which tell listeners how they should interpret the words.[4] Many scholars affirm that more meaning is generated from nonverbal communication than from verbal communication.

---

[3] United Nations Development Programme, *Why Dialogue Matters for Conflict Prevention and Peacebuilding*, February 2009, https://www.undp.org/content/dam/undp/library/crisis%20prevention/dialogue_conflict.pdf.

[4] "Communication Skills for Law Enforcement Officers." Basic Law Enforcement Training Instructor, ppi-inc.net/UserFiles/BLET/i-commsk.pdf.

Body Language

Nonverbal communication refers to the expressions used by people to relay their thoughts, feelings, or emotions without speaking.[5] Nonverbal communication accounts for about 65 percent of meaning that is transmitted between two people during face-to-face communication.[6] An officer who understands nonverbal signals can increase the likelihood of a message being understood correctly; the officer will also be more likely to interpret silent messages and react appropriately.

Nonverbal signals are powerful indicators of what people mean and what they feel. The same words used by one person can mean different things in different situations when accompanied by different gestures and different vocal pitches and tones. Officers may use nonverbal skills to show interest and illustrate that they are paying careful attention to the person with whom they are interacting.[7] Nonverbal communication is about giving physical and psychological attention to another person without exchanging words.

How to Convey Meaning Nonverbally

Eye contact can send messages of support and encouragement, depending on the cultural setting.[8] Gestures also can send messages. For example, drumming one's fingers on a table can signal impatience; crossing one's arms may indicate a closed attitude; and sneaking glances at a watch while listening may relay boredom—messages that might be unintended.

The tone of voice may convey messages that stimulate trust or inspire fear. Tone may also spark anger or misunderstanding—for example, if an officer stops a driver for a traffic offense and says in an exasperated tone,

---

[5] Noel Otu, "Decoding Nonverbal Communication in Law Enforcement," *Salus Journal* 3, no. 2 (2015).

[6] Laura K. Guerrero and Kory Floyd, *Nonverbal Communication in Close Relationships* (Maywah, NJ: Lawrence Erlbaum Associates, 2006).

[7] Neil Katz and Kevin McNulty, "Reflective Listening" (Maxwell School of Citizenship and Public Affairs, Syracuse University, 1994).

[8] Judee K. Burgoon and Thomas P. Saine, *The Unspoken Dialogue: An Introduction to Nonverbal Communication* (Boston: Houghton Mifflin, 1978).

"Don't you get what I am saying?" the driver may think that the officer is calling the driver an idiot. Pace and pitch of spoken words are extremely important in communication between officers and citizens.

Officers communicate nonverbally in a variety of other ways, too, including by the uniform they wear. Adopting a COP ethos requires police to be candid about who they are and what their intentions are. The police uniform is representative of the authority police officers wield. That authority can be seen as legitimate or undeserved based on the conduct of the officer, and the uniform earns a reputation as much as the individual does.

The color of the uniform is an important issue in gaining the trust of the community because the uniform is a sign of power and respect. Police institutions might consider changing from the type of uniform that officers have traditionally worn (especially in countries that have favored military-style uniforms) to more civilian styles of dress.[9] Community members found the full uniforms worn by officers in Cambridge, Massachusetts, intimidating and felt uncomfortable engaging with them as a result. The police department adopted new uniforms (khaki pants and a pullover or a polo shirt emblazoned with the department's logo) so that police would be viewed as more approachable.[10]

Critical Thinking

Critical thinking skills are used in every aspect of policing, and officers should be given the opportunity and space to use their creativity and critical thinking. There is no one textbook answer for every situation, and by encouraging officers to think critically and creatively, they are better equipped to respond to the varied needs of the community they serve.

Police need to think innovatively, especially when they use their discretionary power. They should invoke reason and critical thinking

---

[9] Robert Mauro, "The Constable's New Clothes: Effects of Uniforms on Perceptions and Problems of Police Officers," *Journal of Applied Social Psychology* 14, no. 1 (February 1984): 42–56.

[10] Police Executive Research Forum, *Building Interdisciplinary Partnerships to Prevent Violent Extremism*, Office of Community Oriented Policing Services, 2017.

skills to solve difficult problems.[11] Enhancing police officers' ability to think logically and critically is a vital ingredient in preventing violence and extremism. Empowering officers to think critically teaches them to challenge their biases, false assumptions, and myths.[12] It is a starting point where officers can begin to develop their own worldviews, learn to work collaboratively with others, and appreciate different viewpoints.

Through critical thinking, officers will realize that CVE is not a war with a winner and a loser. When officers put effort into understanding the reasons why some people become alienated and angry enough to join VEOs, police are in a better position to address this problem with the community. Through the use of critical thinking tactics, officers will realize that enforcing the law using militaristic methods is a short-term approach to CVE.

When officers learn and use critical thinking skills, they can better consider the root causes of a problem and come up with new and creative approaches to taking nonviolent and constructive action to prevent and solve that problem. For example, a common approach to investigating a series of burglaries is to tackle each incident individually; this approach, however, does little to address the underlying reason for the crimes being committed. Typically, the investigator will take the statement of a property owner and victim and attempt to find the criminals responsible. If the officer finds the individuals who committed the crime, he or she will arrest them and attempt to return the stolen property. However, an investigator who is equipped with critical thinking skills may move beyond this traditional response and delve into the conditions underlying the spate of burglaries. This may include collecting additional information and attempting to link this incident with other burglaries and conducting an analysis to learn why and how the crimes occurred repeatedly and how they can be prevented.

---

[11] Michael Birzer, "More Effective Training Approach for Contemporary Policing," *Police Quarterly* 4, no. 2 (2001); Wesley Phillips and Darrell Burrell, "Decision-Making Skills That Encompass a Critical Thinking Orientation for Law Enforcement Professionals," *International Journal of Police Science and Management* 11, no. 2 (2009); and Carol Ann Traut, Steve Feimer, Craig Emmert, and Kevin Thom, "Law Enforcement Recruit Training at the State Level: An Evaluation," *Police Quarterly* 3, no. 3 (2000).

[12] Phillips and Burrell, "Decision-Making Skills."

Enforcing the law is one out of many responses to solve such problems, and analysis may indicate the need to tackle the burglaries by involving other partners such as businesses owners, residents, government social services, property managers, and community organizations.

Police institutions need to go beyond reactive, closed, and internal thinking and start thinking more proactively while being open to the community. For example, police officers are often called by business owners to address the issue of homeless individuals who harass customers, panhandle, or sleep on sidewalks and whose presence negatively affects local businesses. These people, who are without a home or regular work, move from place to place and survive by begging for food and cash. A police officer who is taught to follow the letter of the law will be inclined to arrest these people and send them to court. Most of the time, that approach results only in frustration for police and business owners, because the homeless people, after their court date, normally return to do the same things in a different area or even in the same area. The result is that business owners complain again and the whole process restarts. To break out of this cycle, officers could ask themselves why these people are behaving in this manner, what their underlying problems are, and what community resources exist that could help address those problems. Identifying the root causes of behavior can help police identify which government services can help. In this instance, officers could refer homeless individuals to social services that provide job readiness training or access to shelters. If officers research and analyze the problem, they may find long-term solutions for at least some members of this homeless population, addressing their personal issues in addition to the concerns of the business owners and community.

Adopting the COP ethos requires the use of critical thinking skills and problem-solving techniques. Police academies should explore how to teach recruits to think critically to promote good judgment and thus develop reasoning abilities so they can better deal with the complexities of police work. Existing training models emphasize instructor-led activities and consist of a curriculum based on the transference of content from teacher to learner.[13] This instruction model creates recruits who obey orders without

---

[13] M. R. McCoy, "Blackboards and Badges: Teaching Style in Law Enforcement Education and Training in Oklahoma" (doctoral dissertation, Oklahoma State University, Stillwater, 2000).

questioning.[14] Furthermore, this approach teaches recruits to adhere to the "right" answers and avoid trying different approaches. This training environment is not consistent with the mission of today's police officer in the field, which calls for quick thinking and the ability to deploy a variety of skills. Today's officers are expected to operate autonomously, using personal discretion and critical thinking skills to tackle the problems they encounter. The opportunity to practice using critical thinking skills during training is a key element in the development of the capacity to deploy those skills in varied situations in the community.[15]

Because the role of police officers has expanded from law enforcer to problem solver, academy training must move beyond technical training to encompass topics such as problem solving, decision making, and interpersonal communication. Officers should be able to demonstrate sound reasoning, logic, and technical knowledge as they make decisions within seconds of encountering an incident. Asking recruits "what do you think?" may be a starting point for promoting critical thinking, but training programs need to go past that initial step to teach police recruits to analyze and make appropriate decisions on how to respond to a myriad of situations.

Conclusion

Applying COP to CVE efforts requires training that enhances police capacity and equips officers with strong interpersonal and intellectual skills. Communication and critical thinking are crucial in the effort to lower violent extremism in a sustainable manner and to gain the maximum degree of collaboration and support from the community. Using communication skills effectively, officers can better achieve the goals of the police department and encourage the cooperation of community members in efforts to de-escalate situations, rendering use of force less likely in volatile situations.

---

[14] Michael L. Birzer, "Police Training in the 21st Century," *FBI Law Enforcement Bulletin* 68, no. 7 (July 1999): 16–19.

[15] Lisa Gueldenzoph and Mark J. Snyder, "Teaching Critical Thinking and Problem Solving Skills," *Delta Pi Epsilon Journal* 50, no. 2 (2008): 90–99.

CHAPTER 12

CONFLICT RESOLUTION SKILLS

Law enforcement officers are called to handle a variety of conflict situations, in the process performing roles that range from acting as a mediator in a family dispute to controlling violent demonstrations. How an officer responds to incidents depends on his or her experience and skills. Some officers turn a routine traffic stop into a riot whereas some enforce the law and arrest extremely dangerous criminals without inflicting bodily injury; evidently, certain behaviors increase the likelihood of cooperation or violence from the community. An effective and competent officer is able to manage and resolve conflict constructively, deploying conflict resolution skills in tense situations to defuse potential aggression and help identify solutions that satisfy the conflicted parties.

This chapter discusses the importance of conflict resolution skills and the impact of conflict resolution skills on police-individual interactions. It also elaborates on the rationale behind teaching these skills to police officers.

Mediation

Police are often asked to resolve conflicts or to stop a conflict from escalating. Recruits receive some training in mediation, although that precise term may not be used. This section discusses how officers can learn to be effective mediators, how mediation differs from negotiation, and the various roles that officers play during the mediation process.

A practical definition of mediation is the following from the United States Institute of Peace:

> A mode of negotiation in which a mutually acceptable third party helps the parties to a conflict find a solution that they cannot find by themselves. It is a three-sided political process in which the mediator builds and then draws upon relationships with the other two parties to help them reach a settlement. Unlike judges or arbitrators, mediators have no authority to decide the dispute between the parties, although powerful mediators may bring to the table considerable capability to influence the outcome. Mediators are typically from outside the conflict. Sometimes mediators are impartial and neutral, in other cases they have a strategic interest that motivates them to promote a negotiated outcome. Mediators may focus on facilitating communication and negotiation but they also may offer solutions and use leverage, including positive and negative incentives, to persuade the parties to achieve an agreement.[1]

Mediation in the context of policing represents a broad range of activities, including facilitating and setting the stage for resolution, listening to the disputants, and helping them find their own resolutions.[2] Officers mediate to resolve family disputes, conflicts between landlords and tenants, and arguments between residents of a neighborhood (such as issues over driveway access and street parking). Traditional police practices tend to refrain from directly engaging in such disputes except for when

---

[1] Dan Snodderly, *Peace Terms: Glossary of Terms for Conflict Management and Peacebuilding*, 2nd ed. (Washington, DC: United States Institute of Peace Press, 2019), 56.

[2] Michael E. Buerger et al., "Extending the Police Role: Implications of Police Mediation as a Problem-Solving Tool," *Police Quarterly* 2, no. 2 (June 1, 1999): 125–149.

they boil over into the public space. Some scholars describe mediation as a nonconventional conflict resolution method because it does not involve force or arrest, and it is typically underutilized in police work.[3]

The Benefits of Teaching Mediation

Mediation is called for in a variety of conflict situations, and it is a valuable item in the police toolbox that can be used to shape and strengthen police relationships with the community.[4] Officers are usually the first responder in interpersonal disputes. Through the use of mediation, police can resolve disputes and reduce the likelihood that a dispute will escalate or be repeated, which in turn may help improve police-individual relations.[5] Mediation is a practical tool, especially in noncriminal disputes where there are no grounds for arrest or in circumstances where officers must determine whether to issue a citation or make an arrest. For example, although police can arrest persons engaged in a minor physical altercation, mediation may be a more viable and efficient alternative, ensuring that the parties involved do not face jail time, acquire a criminal record, or add to the congestion in courthouses and the overcrowding in jails.

Mediation can reduce the likelihood of escalation. Parties engaged in intense conflict do not communicate effectively and may resort to the use of violence to achieve their goals. The mediation process can establish the conditions to de-escalate the situation and encourage parties to find shared concerns. Occasionally, officers must have separate discussions with each party to encourage them individually to cooperate and to find peaceful solutions. Police using mediation can highlight the benefits of resolving the conflict and the progress being made toward resolution. As a mediator, an officer can create an environment that encourages the conflicting parties to communicate with each other.

---

[3] Christopher Cooper, "Patrol Police Officer Conflict Resolution Processes," *Journal of Criminal Justice* 25, no. 2 (1997): 87–101.

[4] Christopher C. Cooper, "Mediation Training to Improve Police Social Interaction Skills," *Mediate.com*, August 1999.

[5] Christopher C. Cooper, *Conceptualizing Mediation Use by Patrol Police Officers*, Center on Juvenile and Criminal Justice, San Francisco, July 2003.

Mediation allows an officer to learn about some of the issues that lie behind a problem and to encourage people to speak with one another. Mediation entails using a host of skills, including strategic listening, to encourage people to share concerns and explore options for resolving conflict. Sometimes officers can bring underlying issues to the surface through mediation, even if these are not the immediate reasons that the parties claim to be fighting. Underlying issues such as a familial land dispute that occurred years ago can be addressed through a mediated process. Mediation can also help parties to develop a better system of resolving their problem nonviolently.

The mediator helps the parties in conflict empower themselves to find a solution to the dispute. The practice of mediation empowers civilians to determine the outcomes of their conflict; this practice is in direct opposition to the traditional authoritative role of the police officer.[6] Mediation by a police officer represents a transfer of decision-making power from the police officer to the citizen, a process that can lead to individual empowerment. When officers mediate, they give people a chance to communicate their concerns to the police and share their perspectives regarding a particular issue. Empowerment is very important because people want to have control and ownership over the resolution reached, and conflicted parties will feel the solution is a product of their own making if mediation is involved. Ownership of an agreement reached by the parties greatly enhances the chances of it being observed and lasting.[7] This in turn can lead to improved relations between police and the citizenry, because disputing citizens appreciate the empowerment given to them by the mediating officer. Agreements imposed by a police officer and that lack any sense of ownership from those involved are more likely to be breached.[8]

---

[6] Megan Clare Price, "The Process and Partnerships Behind Insight Policing," *Criminal Justice Policy Review* 27, no. 5 (October 13, 2015): 553–567.

[7] Dean Garner Pruitt and Jeffrey Zachary Rubin, *Social Conflict: Escalation, Stalemate, and Settlement* (New York: Random House, 1986).

[8] Ibid.

How to Develop Mediation Skills

Officers need to develop specific skills, such as information gathering and determining the root cause of a problem, to enhance their capacity in mediation. They need to apply communications skills, including asking questions and listening, to gain an in-depth understanding of individual parties' motivations, values, fears, and strengths.

Mediation relies on facilitation skills. The role of a facilitator is not to solve a problem but to help the involved parties identify a mutually beneficial solution. Facilitators start the process of mediation; they close it once a tentative resolution has been reached. Police officers should know how and when to use the art of leverage to address a problem between parties and how to utilize police resources to help the parties change their behavior.

At certain points in the mediation process, officers should explain to the parties their alternatives if mediation fails. The possibility that the officer will arbitrate and decide to send both parties to court can act as an incentive to resolve the issues.[9]

Police officers need engagement skills that enable them to bring together community members who are experiencing conflict with each other. Officers can do that through acknowledging that all parties have the right to their own opinions and engaging with the parties without favoring one or the other. To be an effective mediator, an officer needs solid negotiation skills.

People often use the terms *mediation* and *negotiation* interchangeably, and they do share many common and related elements. When officers use mediation, they negotiate with the parties or help them negotiate with each other. Negotiation is an important component of mediation, yet it is important to understand the differences between the two actions.

Negotiation

Negotiation is a process of communication intended to help conflicted parties work together to shape an outcome that meets their shared interests.

---

[9] Cooper, *Conceptualizing Mediation Use.*

When a party resorts to negotiation, it does so because it recognizes that it cannot obtain the outcome it wants without the buy-in and agreement of one or more other parties For example, when police want to ensure that a demonstration remains peaceful, negotiating with the organizers of the demonstration will probably be more effective than relying on heavy-handed police tactics.

In police work, negotiations take place when there are differences between police and other parties. They occur (or *should* occur) not only when there is a crisis but also during more mundane police interactions. For example, traffic stops are one of the most frequent types of interaction between police officers and the community. When police pull over a driver, they introduce themselves, talk to the driver directly, explain the reason for the stop, listen to anything the driver might say by way of justification or explanation, request the driver's license and clarification of the details, and then decide.[10] During this process, officers are required to use communication skills including listening, speaking, and demonstrating empathy. All these actions and skills are necessary for a police officer to be a good negotiator.[11]

The Benefits of Teaching Negotiation

Negotiation is an important skill for police officers to have, especially for those who interact with the community on a daily basis such as patrol officers, investigators, and traffic police. Police use negotiation to persuade others to buy in to decisions. Learning negotiation skills will improve police interactions with the community and promote trust in the police force.

Negotiation skills are essential for building partnerships and solving problems. Police often have to negotiate with the community about setting priorities, because when it comes to making the community a better and safer place, community members may have different priorities than the local police do. For example, the priority of the police is to

---

[10] Richard R. Johnson, "Citizen Expectations of Police Traffic Stop Behavior," *Policing: An International Journal of Police Strategies & Management* 27, no. 4 (December 2004): 487–497.

[11] Ibid.

fight crime, whereas the priority of the community may concern local and daily considerations such as traffic issues and finding play areas for young people. Strong negotiation skills will assist an officer in identifying common problems and finding effective solutions. Furthermore, when officers practice negotiation, they ensure that community grievances are heard and understood in terms of both their causes and their impacts.

When community members feel that their knowledge is valued, they tend to support and collaborate with police in developing and obtaining funding for local projects, including those that counter the threat of violent extremism. The negotiation regarding what does and does not work to counter violent extremism makes community members feel that they have input into the solution and their voice is heard. Engaging communities with CVE plans creates local buy-in for solutions and demonstrates respect for the community's point of view. Using their negotiation skills, officers can be creative and generate options for agreement that all parties feel are fair solutions.

Sometimes when police perceive a problem being caused by the citizens, officers can display behavior and attitudes that are, or are at least perceived by citizens to be, offensive. In the case of traffic stops, if a police officer displays an offensive attitude or employs harsh policing tactics, a relatively minor traffic violation may escalate to something more serious. Conversely, if an officer uses negotiation and de-escalation techniques during a traffic stop, the situation is more likely to be resolved peacefully. Police can use their negotiation skills to aid their narrative of law enforcement.

In learning negotiation techniques, officers will recognize that relying merely on the law is unhelpful in interactions with the community. They will learn to find and create opportunities and common ground between them and other parties, moving away from laying blame and toward talking about how the officer and citizens can contribute to solving the problem confronting them. Negotiation in policing is ultimately about problem solving, a key component of COP.

Persuasion

Persuasion is required for successful negotiation and mediation and is a critical component of police work. Persuasion is the ability to motivate others to voluntarily observe the law. Persuasion increases an officer's ability to use tactics such as words rather than force and to employ questions rather than orders.

In their engagements with the community, officers often face the challenge of how to persuade effectively: they have to decide which points to raise and in which order, and how to respond to the points raised by community members. To a great extent, the persuasion process is driven by community expectations.[12] For example, if the police want to plan an initiative to address violent extremism but the community expects the police to create a program that addresses a different issue, persuasion is required to convince the community of the merits of the CVE program. Unless a police officer uses persuasion skills to make effective points and articulate a strong argument, the community will think that the police have little to say on the other issue. The community may perceive a lack of police expertise regarding the other issue, and community members will be less willing to collaborate and support the proposed CVE initiative.

Persuasion can be used in a peaceful situations—for example, when creating partnerships—because it increases officers' ability to mobilize others by proving their point in an assertive, confident manner. Persuasion is also essential in crisis situations, and the success of an officer in crisis interactions depends not least on the ability to be persuasive to people in tense situations to gain voluntary compliance.

Police may choose to bully, dictate to, or coerce people to accomplish their objectives, but how successful are those strategies in the long run? When police use persuasion effectively, they gain community collaboration in reaching a shared solution.

Persuasion is different from coercion and different from manipulation. Coercion implies an assumption of compliance, making someone do something by using force or threatening to use force. Manipulation occurs by creating an illusion of free choice to deceive others into making a decision that they might resist under normal circumstances. Persuasion implies no threat or deception but rather the art of making the truth apparent.[13]

[12] Ying Chen and Wojciech Olszewski, "Effective Persuasion," *International Economic Review* 55, no. 2 (April 22, 2014): 319–347.

[13] Sherry Baker and David L. Martinson, "The TARES Test: Five Principles for Ethical Persuasion," *Journal of Mass Media Ethics* 16, no. 2–3 (2001): 148–175.

Persuasion happens when parties feel free to reject the persuasive position; coercion occurs when other parties have constrained choices and they are influenced to act against their preferences.[14]

Officers can incorporate persuasion techniques into their routines to maximize community collaboration. For example, when police respect people and treat them fairly, individuals will be more likely to respond positively. This is known as the "reciprocity principle": people feel indebted to those who do something for them.[15] Furthermore, officers have to rely on facts to support their argument when they propose something. Leaving out key facts of an argument may cause an officer to lose his or her credibility. Using persuasion, officers can establish mutual understanding, motivate compliance, and ultimately negotiate an agreement.

Emotional Intelligence

In their influential book on negotiation, *Getting to Yes,* Roger Fisher, William Ury, and Bruce Patton write, "In a negotiation, particularly in a bitter dispute, feelings may be more important than talk."[16] An awareness of one's emotions and those of other parties is key to success in conflict resolution. Emotional intelligence in this context refers to the ability of the police to understand their own emotions and read the emotional response of others.

Officers should understand the role emotions play in decision making and manage their emotional reactions in all situations. Officers who are emotionally intelligent are more likely to elicit desired results from the involved parties and evaluate risk more accurately, which can result in better decision-making outcomes.[17] Training in emotional intelligence

---

[14] Penny Powers, "Persuasion and Coercion: A Critical Review of Philosophical and Empirical Approaches," *HEC Forum* 19, no. 2 (June 26, 2007): 125–143.

[15] Robert B. Cialdini et al., "Managing Social Norms for Persuasive Impact," *Social Influence* 1, no. 1 (2006): 3–15.

[16] Roger Fisher, William Ury, and Bruce Patton, *Getting to Yes: Negotiating Agreement Without Giving In* (New York: Penguin, 1991).

[17] Ingrid Smithey Fulmer and Bruce Barry, "The Smart Negotiator: Cognitive Ability and Emotional Intelligence in Negotiation," *International Journal of Conflict Management* 15, no. 3 (2004): 245–272.

provides officers with a greater capacity to connect with the community they serve. Emotional intelligence is necessary to build the relationships of trust, cooperation, and collaboration that are necessary to solve community problems.

Developing emotional intelligence starts with the capacity to perceive and express feelings—for example, the ability to decode the messages expressed in facial expressions and tone of voice. [18] Officers should be able to see and understand expressions of fear in the face of other parties. Being aware of such feelings and detecting one's own emotions in response, regulating them as they arise, are part of self-awareness during a negotiation. For example, a police officer who loses control of his or her emotions in a negotiation might confuse the other party, leading to a loss of credibility. Self-awareness is just the start of emotional intelligence, because negotiation is not about ourselves, it is about us interacting with others. Nonetheless, in order to negotiate and connect with people, officers must first gain a thorough understanding of the emotional states inside themselves before attempting to understand the emotions of their counterparts.

Empathy and assertiveness are two elements of emotional intelligence that officers must balance.[19] To be effective negotiators, officers need to be able to respond both empathetically and assertively to others.

Officers might think that empathy is easy to achieve, but in reality, empathy is a challenging skill to develop. An empathetic officer listens carefully to the concerns of others, is sensitive to these concerns, and demonstrates that these concerns are meaningful to the police, providing an opportunity to build trust between parties.[20] Exhibiting empathy makes other parties feel understood and safe enough to participate in a negotiation. Empathy provides the opportunity to understand a person's motivations, preconceptions, and individual needs, allowing an officer to more effectively generate ideas that address the needs of the citizen.

---

[18] H. R. Sacks, "Human Relations Training for Law Students and Lawyers," *Journal of Legal Education* 11 (1959): 316–345.

[19] Robert H. Mnookin et al., "The Tension Between Empathy and Assertiveness," *Negotiation Journal* 12, no. 3 (1996): 217–230.

[20] Bilyana Martinovski et al. "Rejection of Empathy in Negotiation," *Group Decision and Negotiation* 16, no. 1 (December 16, 2006): 61–76.

Yet too much empathy makes an officer ineffective. Officers may forget to advocate for their own needs or the needs of the law. They may feel obligated to agree to whatever people ask of them, and they may not be able to articulate reciprocal requests.

Assertiveness is also an important skill for officers to develop. Officers should not lose sight of the fact that they are in a negotiation to assert their police force's needs. However, too much assertiveness leads community members to feel that the police force is bullying them and that the officer they are talking to does not care about their individual concerns.

Simulated negotiation exercises provide opportunities to transform the concepts and principles of emotional intelligence from theory into practice. Training should be provided to police officers on how to determine why they feel the way they do, how to express those emotions, and how to use this information in making more informed decisions. Police academies and trainers should consider emotional intelligence a vital part of the training as they work to develop their recruits' negotiation skills.

Approaches to Conflict Resolution

How officers approach a conflict informs the outcome. Some researchers suggest that there are five conflict styles that sit along a spectrum: competition, avoidance, accommodation, compromise, and collaboration and problem solving.[21] Officers need to be able to assess a situation by identifying the conflict style of those involved and to adapt their engagement accordingly.

Officers need to plan how they will handle a negotiation. Will the officer begin by giving the other party something it wants—by accommodating—as a way to build trust, or will he or she use another approach? Officers may use a series of different styles when negotiating a solution to a problem or conflict. They may move from one approach to another as the negotiation evolves. What is important here is to be flexible, adaptable, and responsive to the situation.

---

[21] C. Runde and T. Flanagan, *Developing your Conflict Competence* (San Francisco: Jossey Bass, 2011).]

Officer should understand strategies of "win-win" and "win-lose." [22] Win-win negotiations are where both parties end the negotiation feeling that they gained something that they wanted, even if it is not everything that they had hoped for, so that they are satisfied with the solution. Win-lose strategies indicate competition between police and the community; in using a win-lose approach, one party aims to defeat their other, often leading to escalation of the conflict as losers try to retaliate against the winners. Adopting the COP ethos requires police to undertake a strategy of collaborative partnerships among law enforcement and the communities they serve to promote trust; the win-win approach will foster meaningful and strong relationships with the community. By using a win-win strategy, police officers focus on reaching shared, broadly acceptable outcomes, not on achieving narrowly conceived ones that satisfy only the police department.[23] Win-lose strategies promote an us-versus-them mentality and can lead police to behave contrary to the will of the community; relationships often become adversarial rather than collaborative.

The first principle of conflict resolution is to separate the parties from the problem. Officers tend to become personally involved with issues and with their side's positions. They will tend to interpret the other party's responses as personal attacks. Separating the people from the issues allows all parties to address the issues without damaging their relationship.

The second principle is to pay attention to interests, not positions. Officers should focus on the underlying rather than the immediate reasons for a conflict. This approach allows the officer to address the root cause of the problem.

The third principle is to generate options—to think about different ways that a conflict can be resolved. Officers should not get stuck on a solution that does not work or resonate with the audience. They should bring other ideas to the table. Reaching out to people who have had similar problems to see if they have a possible solution might be advisable.

---

[22] Roger Fisher, William Ury, and Brice Patton, *Getting to Yes: Negotiating Agreement without Giving In* (Boston, New York: Houghton Mifflin, Boston, i1991).,

[23] Alejandro Beutel and Peter Weinberger, *Public-Private Partnerships to Counter Violent Extremism: Field Principles for Action* (National Consortium for the Study of Terrorism and Responses to Terrorism, College Park, MD, July 2016).

Conclusion

Conflict resolution skills are critical components of police work even though they are not included in many existing police academy training programs. Police institutions that are serious about adopting a COP ethos should make conflict resolution skills a standard part of their academy curricula. Officers should be able to practice the skills required for community policing after they graduate from the academy. Effective officers utilize appropriate conflict resolution skills to prevent situations from escalating. A lack of communication skills can lead to verbal confrontation between officers and individuals and may lead to physical confrontations that ignite and exacerbate community hostility. Acquiring communication skills will help foster positive police-community interactions, empower citizens, and encourage cooperation throughout the community. Because they help build trusted relationships, conflict resolution skills help police nurture collaborative partnerships with the community. Negotiations and mediations are opportunities for the police to work with communities to identify their needs and problems, and to jointly develop and implement solutions.

CHAPTER 13
INFORMAL TRAINING

Many police academies focus on learning outcomes from formal instruction only. However, there is an opportunity to reinforce that training with *in*formal education (i.e., activities conducted and messages delivered during the hours before and after formal instruction). An academy that embraces the significant changes in the formal curriculum recommended in this book may still not be able to fully embrace the COP ethos unless it also changes the informal training it provides.

This chapter looks first at the problems associated with sending one sort of message to recruits via formal lessons and another during informal training. It then spotlights the militarized environment within which much informal (and formal) training occurs. The last section of the chapter discusses the importance of academy instructors and police leadership modelling the kind of behavior that will support, rather than undermine, a COP ethos.

Sending Contradictory Messages

Police academy training consists not only of what recruits are taught in the classroom, but also of the many hours that recruits spend outside the classroom, during which they may interact with each other and their instructors in various ways, including by debating and analyzing the content presented to them through formal instruction. While the formal and informal messages can be sometimes by complementary, much of the time they are inconsistent—often significantly so.[1] The reinforcement of key training messages are meant to manifest themselves in a shift in mindset and to create a way of understanding the role of police in society.[2] When formal and informal lessons do not support and reinforce each other, the learning outcomes of formal training are much less likely to be integrated by officers. The formal curriculum proposed in this book emphasizes an outward-looking approach to policing and working proactively with the community to solve problems. Informal lessons should reinforce these principles rather than undermine them.

Formal and informal training function together provide recruits with skills, knowledge, and attitudes that they take with them into the police force. Formal training is planned and structured, with learning objectives approved by the head of the training academy. Informal training is often referred to as "learning by experience" and has no objective in terms of learning outcomes.[3] Formal training may teach recruits about how to respect diversity in the society, while informal lessons might reinforce gendered or ethnic stereotypes through an overemphasis on masculine characteristics such as physical strength.[4] These inequalities and biases will be carried from the academy to the field, and officers will be likely to exhibit learned or inherent prejudices when dealing with the community. Contradictory lessons between class-based training and extracurricular activities are destructive to the COP ethos and put recruits in a moral dilemma: should they follow the formal instructions of training or the informal rules reinforced by the behavior of their instructors?

---

[1] Robert E. Ford, "Saying One Thing, Meaning Another: The Role of Parables in Police Training," *Police Quarterly* 6, no. 1 (March 1, 2003): 84–110.

[2] Citlali Alexandra Déverge, "Police Education and Training: A Comparative Analysis of Law Enforcement Preparation in the United States and Canada" (master's thesis, University of Southern Mississippi, 2016).

[3] Jay Liebowitz and Michael S. Frank, *Knowledge Management and e-Learning* (Boca Raton, FL: CRC Press, 2011).

[4] Nancy Marion, "Police Academy Training: Are We Teaching Recruits What They Need to Know?" *Policing: An International Journal of Police Strategies & Management* 21, no. 1 (1998): 54–79.

A Militarized Environment

The police academy environment puts stress on recruits both emotionally and physically by subjecting them to extensive and rigid rules and regulations. Recruits are told to obey orders and rules unquestioningly. The day the new recruit walks through the door of the academy, he or she is asked to leave behind the community and personal liberties, and to submit to the authority of the institution.[5] Immediately after arrival, male recruits receive a hair cut in a military fashion.

This military style runs throughout the typical day for a trainee at the academy.

The day begins when the coordinator wakes recruits up. Officers in training are expected to be dressed, with beds made, and in formation outside of their buildings, ready to begin daily physical exercises, fifteen minutes after their wakeup call. Once the recruits are lined up, they sing songs that emphasize the strength and might of the police service. They are inspected to ensure that they are dressed appropriately and that their uniforms are clean, ironed, tucked in, and generally presentable. Recruits then take part in physical exercises and marching drills, before attending classes on police history, rules and law, and other law enforcement topics (see chapter 5). They are required to stand at attention when a ranking officer walks by. During breaks for meals, recruits follow specific rules in the mess hall, such as being silent and eating quickly while the coordinator (who deals with discipline issues and sometimes substitutes for teachers)[6] supervises the mess hall and punishes anyone who breaks the rules.

After formal lessons, which last on average eight hours a day, cadets are taken back to their rooms. The academy coordinator may call on them before dinner to perform additional physical exercises or make a presentation. Staff members assigned to supervise and coordinate recruit activities may use physical discipline, additional work assignments, or verbal harassment as punishment for unacceptable conduct or misbehavior. They may reprimand the recruit harshly without indicating how they would have preferred the recruit to behave or act. Punishment may include pushups, in keeping with the military atmosphere. After dinner, recruits

---

[5] Chappell and Lanza-Kaduce, "Police Academy Socialization."
[6] Chappell and Lanza-Kaduce, "Police Academy Socialization."

are taken back to their rooms, where they spend the evening cleaning their rooms, organizing their lockers, folding clothes, and finally sleeping.

According to leadership, this demanding hierarchical structure develops an adherence to discipline and fosters a sense of solidarity among the recruits, preparing them for their work in the field. However, the ways in which rules are enforced, and the exacting physical standards set, send the message that, outside the academy, community members should be dealt with in a similar manner.

Modelling the COP Ethos

The behavior modeled by police superiors and academy instructors has a significant impact on recruits, shaping their understanding of the norms, values, and conduct that they should embrace or display as a police officer. Recruits observe the way—in terms of what is said and not said, and the tone of voice and body language used—that instructors and higher-ranking officers treat each other, treat lower-ranking officers, and treat the recruits themselves. Once they leave the academy, the new officers watch how their colleagues and superiors treat members of the communities they are meant to protect. Those who do not model fairness and collaboration exacerbate the culture and mindset of violence and coercion that has traditionally underpinned policing as a profession. But those who model respect, share insights, and always seek out opportunities to learn help to shift the culture toward a COP ethos.

The effectiveness of community-oriented training relies on instructors and their commitment to the COP ethos.[7] Many instructors are retired or active police officers who are chosen for their experience in the field and their interest in the training.[8] But in some instances, assignment to the training academy as an instructor has been seen as a sign of official disfavor; trainers have been selected because they have performed poorly in the field. Unsurprisingly, trainers selected on this basis have not always

---

[7] A. T. Chappell and L. Lanza-Kaduce, "Integrating Sociological Research with Community-Oriented Policing: Bridging the Gap Between Academics and Practice," *Journal of Applied Sociology/Sociological Practice* 21, no. 6 (2004): 80–98.

[8] Marion, "Police Academy Training."

brought a positive and collaborative spirit to their role as instructors. Academy leadership that wants to instill a COP ethos in recruits should pay attention to the selection process for instructors and improve instructor recruitment and instructor evaluation. Instructors must be expected to model the same behaviors that they want recruits to exhibit when they interact with the public. They should have strong communication and presentation skills and should advocate the COP ethos at all times on duty. If instructors do not buy into the COP ethos, recruits will not accept the idea of the COP.

Conclusion

Simply changing the training curriculum is not sufficient to incorporate a COP ethos into police activities. Significant changes in informal training are also required. When the messages of COP are reinforced through informal discussions and interactions between recruits and academy instructors, the tenets of COP are more likely to be retained and reflected in the behavior of recruits when they start work as officers. Police academies should recognize that the informal academy experience is as important as formal training to behavioral outcomes.[9]

Police academies can develop policies for all types of learning, including both formal and informal lessons, and find ways to align informal instruction with the formal curriculum. Instructors can revisit and expand on the need to listen strategically to members of the community by modeling strategic listening during more personal and relaxed exchanges between new recruits. In the classroom and in casual conversations outside the classroom, good practice in interacting with community members can be emphasized.

Humiliation, verbal abuse, harassment, and physical exercise as punishment should have no place in the training environment. Police academy training programs must examine the impact of bureaucracy and hierarchy on the mindset that officers develop. The police academy mission statement should reflect the COP philosophy and represent its

---

[9] Richard J. Lundman, *Police and Policing: An Introduction* (New York: Holt, Rinehart and Winston, 1980).

values throughout the entire training program and learning process. The academy might consider giving more emphasis to horizontal authority relationships and less to vertical relationships so as to sensitize recruits to the horizontal relationships that officers will encounter in community policing activities. This means an increased emphasis on joint problem solving across professional lines, as opposed to a hierarchical model in which the opinion of superiors always holds sway.

PART V

CONCLUSION

CHAPTER 14
IMPACT OF PROPOSED CURRICULUM

Over the past two decades, law enforcement institutions have expanded their power to counter the threat of violent extremism, and police have come to play a crucial role in this endeavor. This expanded power has often resulted in police relying purely on the use of intimidation and force to emphasize the authority of law enforcement. Excessive use of force by police is often criticized by the public, making police appear less accountable to their community and in turn undermining police efforts to establish collaborative relationships with the public. A militaristic approach to policing to address the threat of violent extremism makes police officers nearly indistinguishable from soldiers in certain contexts; heavily armed with weaponry and protective gear, the police literally and figuratively distance themselves from the general public.

Current police training programs do not prepare recruits for a COP ethos. The prevalence of heavy-handed tactics has a negative impact on the efforts of police—more aggressive tools translate into more aggressive policing. Heavy-handed policing involving covert operations, surveillance, and intelligence gathering may contribute to erase the trust that police have sometimes spent years trying to build and can erode collaboration between the public and police in the fight against violent extremism.

Misplaced and unnecessary heavy-handed policing is more likely to produce grievances, rouse anger, and escalate violence than to counter violent extremism. Employing hard policing tactics may be justified as a short-term attempt to reassure a scared public but it may often give rise to additional grievances that could in turn fuel yet more violence. Use of force as a primary tool to handle RLVE and other criminality could increase community resistance and hostility toward the police, does not promote voluntary compliance, and discourages cooperation with police. In fact, the community will be reluctant and less motivated to inform police about any suspicious activities that might assist in their ability to prevent RLVE. In short, the unnecessary use of hard policing tactics may undermine the basis of trust between the police and community.

If COP is to be an effective CVE strategy, COP must encompass consideration of the effects of coercive policies and practices on the people that violent extremists seek to engage. Adopting a COP ethos requires police to move away from the traditional approach of reporting and arresting criminals and focus instead on mitigation and prevention. This evolution in policing practices takes into consideration the root causes of issues that may arise in the community. COP in the context of violent extremism addresses the factors that contribute to the justification of violent extremist groups, introducing dynamics between the police and the people they protect that privileges longstanding communication and collaboration.

Embracing COP enables police and the community to anticipate problems and work collaboratively to solve them. COP is distinct from other approaches to policing, such as intelligence-led policing, which involves police interacting with the community solely through the use of surveillance technology and informants. Instead, COP emphasizes community collaboration and partnership building. By providing services that reflect the needs of the community and exhibit a tolerance for diversity, police will positively contribute to addressing the root causes of conflict in society.

The COP ethos is not only a tactic or program-specific procedure; it is a philosophical approach to how policing should be carried out. It is an ethos that should be adopted by the entire agency and feed into all police activities. Creating a special unit or assigning a community policing officer to one neighborhood are not appropriate methods for translating this ethos into practice. To enjoy the full benefit of adopting the COP ethos, the entire department (the police system and individual police officers) must embrace it.

COP is made up of three components: problem solving, partnerships, and organizational transformation. When police and the community engage in the proactive and systematic examination of identified problems, they develop and evaluate effective solutions. Effective community partnerships enable the police to understand issues and remain informed so that potential interventions can be conducted early and locally, before problems escalate. Organizational transformation addresses the alignment of management, structure, personnel, and information systems to support community partnerships and proactive problem solving.

This publication discusses the benefits of adopting the COP ethos to counter violent extremism and the obstacles that impede its success. Adopting the COP ethos can mitigate the factors that lead to radicalization. In COP, police have a significant prevention capacity and are close to the community. This proximity to the community allows officers to identify symptoms of RLVE and recognize the factors that may draw vulnerable people to join violent extremist groups. Working together, police and the community can help prevent further radicalization of those who teeter on the fence. Police collaboration with local partners (including community faith leaders, political and social leaders, refugees, and health centers and education services) with the intention of building long-term relationships, can better equip officers to positively react to potential signs of anti-social behaviors, and encourage community members to feel comfortable reporting potential suspicious activity related to violent extremism or other crimes. Police officers who are assigned in a fixed geographic area for an extended period of time are likely to develop deep, long-lasting relationships that foster communication and partnership between police and members of the community.

Challenges of Adopting COP

Adopting the COP ethos is no easy task. There are many challenges, ranging from institutional to individual ones. The structural organization of many police departments is quasi-military, based on a centralized authority with a few managers in charge of decision making, operations, and activities. For many police officers, policing is about fighting and investigating crime rather than forging partnerships and solving problems. COP in the context of violent extremism may be perceived as a way to gather information to counter terrorism. Different understandings of the values and meaning of COP have made it mean different things to different people.

Many police departments claim to have adopted a COP approach and problem-oriented policing practices that rely less on physical skills and the use of force. Yet, the roles and responsibilities of police officers under a COP philosophy differ from those in a traditional policing structure, and existing training programs have proved insufficient to address the underlying causes of violent extremism and other crimes that COP strives to address. COP requires a critical change in the training curriculum as well as a change in how it is delivered.

The Need for a New Paradigm

A new curriculum that promotes critical thinking and problem-solving capacity is needed to implement a COP ethos. Many police academies and departments continue to operate as bureaucratic and militaristic organizations, as manifested in a focus on tactical skills such as the use of force, drills, and first aid rather than skills related to community and problem-oriented policing. No international standard for the content of training exists, and there is no agreement about what sort of curriculum will produce an effective, unbiased, and professional police officer. In each country, police leadership determines the content of the training curriculum. The length of the training program similarly varies from country to country, although typically training for recruits encompasses anywhere from 450 to 600 hours spread over 12 to 18 weeks.

Training has many effects on police behavior and, eventually, on the community. The gaps in training identified in this book may negatively impact the behavior of police officers and impair their ability to learn about problems that may lead to grievances if not addressed effectively. Typical police academy training creates a heavy-handed police mentality. Officers focus on their personal safety over the safety of the citizens with whom they come into contact. Existing training creates a police culture centered on traditional law enforcement practices that can fuel community grievances and reinforce extremist messages. Furthermore, typical training does not prepare officers to respond effectively and professionally to the needs and concerns of the community. Although modern police spend increasing amounts of time responding to issues not necessarily criminal in nature, problem-solving and interpersonal skills are still a low priority on the training agenda.

Standard police academy training impedes the development of trust in police institutions. The use of force is presented as the easiest and most effective way to solve problems despite the fact that most of the calls to police are made by people hoping to resolve problems or obtain information about social services, situations that are not directly or necessarily criminal in nature and that do not involve violence or require the use of force.

Ideally, law enforcement services are carefully and comprehensively trained to be able to contribute to CVE goals. The current training content, however, does not build officers' capacity to partner and solve problems with the communities they serve, leaving police ineffective at addressing the threat of violent extremism. Traditional police measures and interventions such as heavy-handed tactics and surveillance are not enough to respond to this threat.

Police Serve the Community

This book provides an assessment of current police training in an attempt to determine if it effectively prepares officers for their entry into the field in a COP organization. Police officers who are taught only laws and heavy-handed tactics risk overlooking a key policing principle, which is to serve and protect the community. Citizens see police officers carrying heavy weaponry, driving in armored vehicles, and wearing bulletproof vests and helmets—they would look more at a home on a battlefield than in the streets of a community. The current emphasis on physical training and the manifestation of this emphasis in the community is extremely dangerous for the relationship between civilians and police forces. Officers may not be concerned about preempting violence, instead focusing on responding to immediate criminal activity and arresting perpetrators. Although police must work within the community, they are trained to view community members as hostile threats and to respond to real and perceived risks with violent measures.

Basic training shapes the police force and should equip officers with skills to serve and protect the community. An assessment of current training indicates that gaps exist and training modules do not meet the educational and training objectives of a police force that strives for a COP ethos. Academies must shift toward a more thorough curriculum that teaches broader skills. Courses should teach recruits to address the root causes of crime and violent extremism, understand human behavior, appreciate the diversity of the community, and apply communication and other conflict resolution skills. COP requires all officers to adopt empathetic perspectives and communication skills. These courses could be taught in lieu of topics such as infantry training and certain criminal laws; shortening the length of other modules—for example, reducing the time allocated for weaponry training and defensive tactics—will allow more time for recruits to acquire skills and knowledge that are more valuable within a COP context.

By restructuring current training and providing an in-depth understanding of the role of police in the community, officers will gain a stronger awareness of how their words and actions may be received by community members. Ongoing training that focuses on problem solving and creating partnerships is required to ensure effective interactions with the wide range of people an officer may come into contact with.

Police officers should be trained to use every encounter to build community trust and confidence in the police. Public consent and support of law enforcement are two of the most valuable tools in a police officer's kit. Understanding the importance of public confidence and how police can raise the level of confidence through their actions and behavior vis-à-vis the public will increase people's willingness to operate with police both in the sense of voluntary compliance with the law as well as in coming forward to report problems in the community. Officers should understand and apply the concept of procedural justice and realize that insofar as they model fairness in their interactions with community members, community confidence in the police will grow. All these steps will enhance a positive public image of the police.

Crime is primarily the result of social and economic inequalities. To prevent crime, it is important for police officers to understand its roots. Armed with this knowledge, officers can proactively address areas of local anxiety, taking appropriate measures to provide resources and strengthen the sense of community to reduce the likelihood of criminal or violent activity. Teaching officers the root causes of crime and violence gives them the opportunity to gain a more robust comprehension of the various factors that may lead an individual down a violent path. When officers understand and recognize the factors that lead to crime, they are better able to shape interventions and to redirect resources or individuals before the opportunity for violence presents itself. Understanding the root causes of violence is extremely important for COP.

Police officers should recognize that they serve societies that are increasingly more diverse. Many nationalities, cultures, and religious beliefs may coexist within one community. Respecting and acknowledging differences is important to building trust and mutual respect between police and the community. Providing officers with knowledge and skills to identify their biases will help them relinquish prejudices and abandon false stereotypes. Teaching officers about their unconscious, preconceived notions of what it means to be "other" will help them treat all members of the community with respect. It will also eventually eliminate discriminatory ethnic profiling and contribute to a willingness to communicate with all segments of the community. This in turn will help repair police-community relations, particularly with minorities, reinforcing the concept of partnership.

Under the training paradigm recommended here, officers will better understand the multiple ways in which individuals identify and represent themselves, which will help officers to respond in a fair and just way to calls for service from all demographics. In acting in a way that is free from discrimination, officers will be viewed as fair and just service providers, worthy of partnering efforts and able to tailor their responses to the diverse needs of their community.

Skills such as communication, problem solving, and critical thinking build capacity to develop a more community-centric approach that will enhance government efforts in regard to CVE. Through communication and collaboration, police officers and the people they serve can tailor initiatives to address specific, shared needs and concerns and help foster the common purpose of keeping communities safe. These skills are a good starting point for relying on the capacity of individual officers in exercising discretion to remain on the nonlethal side of the continuum of force as much as possible. In doing so, officers will be able to establish collaborative partnerships within their communities. These skills will increase the capacity of police officers to build and use these partnerships to proactively address public safety concerns and develop strategies to identify, prevent, and mitigate the drivers of violent extremism.

A Modern Approach

Applying COP to CVE efforts requires a new approach to police training that aims to enhance police capacity and equip officers with outreach skills. The goal of the police academy is to give recruits a range of tools to enforce the law and prevent conflict. Communication skills are a powerful law enforcement tool and a crucial methods for building partnerships and solving problems. Police officers need to learn skills such as strategic listening, reading body language, effective communication, and critical thinking to employ innovative approaches to the problems encounter. These skills can be used to gain collaboration and support from the community and reduce levels of violent extremism in a sustainable manner. They may also aid police in refraining from using force in tense situations.

Police academies spend little time discussing the importance of de-escalation tactics for dealing with mentally ill persons, homeless persons, and other challenging situations. Conflict resolution skills such as mediation and negotiation will help officers respond to such situations and assist them in shaping and strengthening their relationship with the community. Officers who are well versed in these skill sets will encourage conflicting parties to find peaceful resolutions, thereby reducing the likelihood of violent escalation.

Empowering frontline officers by providing them with opportunities to learn new skills such as facilitation, setting the stage for mediation, and listening to disputants will help them identify and prioritize problems and make decisions on how to best solve them. For example, giving members of the public the opportunity to address their grievances, which may also be the drivers of violent extremism, can help community members feel empowered and engaged. Engaged community members are an invaluable asset for police forces working to defeat violent extremism.

* * *

This book has been developed to guide efforts to incorporate the knowledge and skills necessary for police operations to embrace COP. Integrating the modules suggested here into the training of police academies will enhance the capacity of the police to proactively solve problems, develop partnerships with the community, and respond professionally to requests for help. It is recommended that police academies adopt the training content presented in this book to assist police departments to act as credible and legitimate service providers, thereby making a vital contribution to their country's CVE capacity.

www.ingramcontent.com/pod-product-compliance
Lightning Source LLC
Chambersburg PA
CBHW032000190326
41520CB00007B/303